BEARING PRECIOUS SEED

Eric Casto

WESTBOW
PRESS®
A DIVISION OF THOMAS NELSON
& ZONDERVAN

WestBow Press books may be ordered through booksellers or by contacting:

WestBow Press
A Division of Thomas Nelson & Zondervan
1663 Liberty Drive
Bloomington, IN 47403
www.westbowpress.com
1 (866) 928-1240

All Scripture quotations are taken from the King James Version.

Front Cover Photo Compliments of Richard Ware - UK

ISBN: 978-1-9736-6552-6 (sc)
ISBN: 978-1-9736-6553-3 (hc)
ISBN: 978-1-9736-6551-9 (e)

Library of Congress Control Number: 2019907354

Print information available on the last page.

WestBow Press rev. date: 06/25/2019

Dedication

To my wife, Beth, my greatest friend.
Through great trials, you stood strong and
were a rock I could lean on. I love you.

To my parents, William and Priscilla
Casto, who taught me what it meant to
have faith in God. With faith in God, they
taught me to love foreign missions.

To my children, Caleb, Kelsey, and Victoria.
Having you three with your mother and me
on the mission field was truly a great joy. The
testimonies in this book are a part of your heritage.

To Eve, the girl on the school bus. Because
of your faithfulness in witnessing to Beth
and of course by giving her a gospel tract,
you are in many ways a part of this book.

Also, a big thank you to "Dad" Hague. Your
encouragement and proof-reading were invaluable.

Special thanks to our partners and friends who have
stood with us throughout many years. There is a
harvest of souls and great reward for you in Heaven.

ACKNOWLEDGEMENTS

In honor of the late Pastor Billy Joe Daugherty, Victory Christian Center, Tulsa, Oklahoma. His love for ORU students, evangelism, and foreign missions left an eternal mark on us. It was during those early years of being missionaries in England that his encouragement, whether by phone or by mail, was invaluable.

Alistair and Connie Scott, you both have been such a blessing. Your support and friendship have been of immeasurable value.

Last, I would like to say thank you to Pastor Colin Urquhart and the Kingdom Faith Church and Bible College. This book carries so many wonderful testimonies that belong to you and the tremendous teams that you have afforded this venture. Words cannot express our love for you and the love for revival that you carry.

CONTENTS

INTRODUCTION

God created seed. Seed carries an attribute of God, and that attribute is the power of life. When God created man, He blessed him and gave him authority to have dominion and to subdue the earth. With this empowerment, God then introduced man to seed. Seed carries in it the power of resurrection and multiplication. Without seed, man cannot subdue the earth.

I am writing this book to encourage you, the reader, whoever you are and wherever you live. God knows where you are and He sees what you do for His kingdom. Never be discouraged, though there are seasons of temptation, but always rise up and stir up the gift that God has placed inside of you. You are the light of this world, a city on a hill that shall never be hidden. You have been empowered to overcome impossibilities through the power of seed-time and harvest. Rise up and plant, and as you do, resurrection life shall be released into the earth. In doing so, you shall bring forth a mighty harvest for the Lord.

WHILE THE EARTH REMAINS,
SEEDTIME AND HARVEST,
AND COLD AND HEAT, AND
SUMMER AND WINTER, AND
DAY AND NIGHT SHALL NOT
CEASE
GENESIS 8:22

CHAPTER 1
GOD BIRTHS MISSIONARIES

In the early to mid-nineties, I was given the tremendous opportunity of working as a staff minister at Faith Landmarks Ministries, a dynamic church in Richmond, Virginia. Beth and I had graduated from Oral Roberts University in December 1991 and were married in March 1992. In 1993 I was hired as a staff minister, and over the next few years we watched God move in and through a local congregation that touched its community as well as the nations of the world. The years serving that wonderful church family were not only life-changing but were filled with great excitement. It was truly like riding on the nose of a bullet.

Beth and I have always had a heart for the mission field. While studying at Oral Roberts University, we were faithfully involved in weekend evangelistic outreaches, and during our summer breaks we would invest our lives into mission trips. These trips were extremely important steps pertaining to the calling and direction of God upon our lives.

This journey of the FourSmiles CrossWalk began in 1995 when my pastor sent me to Bangalore, India, to set up an evangelistic open-air meeting in that city. En route to India, I was forced into a layover at London's Heathrow Airport for fifteen hours. Everything about me hated the thought of an extremely long layover, but I couldn't help noticing that my spirit was so joyfully stirred about being in London. After walking around the terminal for an hour, I found a place to sit and stare out across the tarmac and watch the planes land. These planes were coming in from all over the world. As I gazed out at the horizon, I knew that something special was happening in me. However, like most seeds when planted, there was nothing visible. In fact, in my case, everything appeared the same as it did before the seed was planted. The seed of an apple tree looks exactly like the seed of a cherry tree after they are planted. They both are invisible to the human eye. Though unseen on the surface, something miraculous happens just inches beneath the soil that will grow, become visible, and one day produce an abundance of fruit.

After many trips to and from India, passing through London each time, the stage was set for the next step. Upon the completion of our church's mission to India, my pastor approached me about setting up a gospel meeting in central London. At the time I was so busy with my responsibilities at the church that I didn't have much time to consider what was growing in my heart. I was like the pregnant lady who didn't know she was pregnant. A seed had been placed in my spirit, and it was slowly growing. Even though I was extremely happy with my job at the church, I couldn't help noticing that something was different in me. Something was growing in me, and every day I was becoming, in a good way, more uncomfortable.

I was now en route back overseas but this time to work in London. The meetings were to be held for two nights at the historic Methodist Central Hall just next to the beautiful Westminster Abbey. This trip was unlike any other trip I had experienced. The joy that I had in my spirit while walking around Westminster was tremendous.

Back at home, my pastor was so moved in his heart concerning Great Britain that he presented to the congregation a vision of planting a ministry base in London. The church began hiring lawyers in order to legally create a charity in the UK that would oversee the vision of the ministry. There were times that our pastor operated in ministry like a prophet. When he talked about London, it was undeniable that he was speaking prophetically about the purposes of God. He would wait on the Lord and then move with the winds of the Holy Spirit in order to establish God's ideas in the earth. In this prophetic juncture, God was planting a ministry into Europe from the spiritual mountain of Faith Landmarks.

Even though I so enjoyed being in Britain, I purposefully ignored what was happening in me in order to stay focused on my job responsibilities at the church. At that time, I was running a full-time youth ministry and Bible school called DTS, which was preparing teenagers for future purpose and Christian missions. I was also working on laying the foundation for the church's media department which eventually would become a television ministry. I had no time to think about moving to England. When my pastor talked to the congregation about the new ministry base being established in London, my own father-in-law told me later that his spirit was so stirred within him. God was already preparing our family members concerning our upcoming move.

At that particular time, I didn't need to entertain thoughts about the UK because our church was now in the process of moving two missionaries out of Russia to oversee this new ministry endeavor. Concerning the UK, my job was very simple: I was to set up the London Ablaze meeting and then organize and care for the church support team that would travel to England.

God's Glory and the Map of Britain

In 1996 I traveled "across the pond" several times in order to ensure that everything was moving forward for the meetings at Methodist Central Hall. On one particular Sunday evening while working in London, I decided to attend a revival meeting at Kensington Temple Church. Kensington Temple was originally established by the healing evangelist George Jeffreys in the 1930's. I traveled to the area of North Acton to attend an evening worship service at their secondary location. At the time, the church was so big they needed another venue in order to host the whole congregation. As the train arrived at the North Acton station, I began to sense a tangible presence of the Lord. I never knew that the presence of the Lord could canopy an area like that. Needless to say, my heart was being energized with such expectancy.

After stepping off the train, I was soon joined by hundreds of people heading to the meeting. During the worship that night the presence of God fell like rain. It was in that glorious worship that I had a vision. I saw the map of the United Kingdom and in the heart of the nation I saw spokes of fire going out to the ends of the earth. Then a strong "knowing" came over me that we were to position ourselves in Britain for this operation of the Spirit of God. I saw an outpouring of the Holy Spirit that went out to the nations from Great Britain, and with this vision, I received a commission to come and be a part of it.

My world was being turned upside down, and I was trying to figure it all out. At the same time, I was working in another man's ministry whose vision did not include my moving to Great Britain. Because of this, I kept pushing it all down so that I could stay focused on the tasks at hand. I simply prayed, "Lord, I will never say no to you, but in this case, you will have to work out these details."

When the time finally came for the London Ablaze meetings, there was great excitement among our church team members. London is such a beautiful city—a city at the heart of the British Empire, whose influence touched the ends of the earth. Because of the British Empire, London is still a world capital. The nations of the world live there and pass through her streets on a daily basis. A ministry in London has the potential to reach the four corners of the globe.

With the team's excitement came the need to channel it so that expectancy would continue to remain high. Thus, the idea emerged to do street evangelism in hopes of inviting people to the meetings. I took the church team of Americans out onto the streets and we handed out tracts and flyers and attempted to share the love of Jesus with people. This was my first experience doing street ministry in London, and it was one of the hardest things I had ever experienced. Though it was hard at the time, however, I had no idea that God was laying a foundation in me for what was to come.

Upon returning to the USA, Beth and I continued to find ourselves stirred in our spirits and increasingly dissatisfied; that is, a dissatisfaction that pertained to God's purpose upon our lives. We were very busy; the local church in Richmond was growing, and we were seeing success at every turn. The church, although it was several thousand members, operated like a family, and the corporate faith was strong. It is very hard to want to leave a church like that.

Jesus Is Here

One Saturday, Beth and I were sitting in the living room in our little house talking about what was happening in our hearts. As we began sharing with one another, the atmosphere in the room changed. Beth looked at me and very quietly announced, "Jesus is here." When she said that, I was overwhelmed by His presence, and I knew that He was standing next to me. Though we did not see Him with our eyes, His glory permeated us. In that moment, these words came: "Separate unto the work I have called you to." Now the Lord's will was clear, and we would have to make a faith step into this new direction.

The following week after this experience, I was called into a staff meeting with my pastor. Because there were so many changes happening at the church due to growth and the expansion of vision, he wanted to adjust my job responsibilities. As we discussed the new workload I grew more and more restless inside. I couldn't hold back any longer, so I briefly closed my eyes and stepped out in faith. I interrupted the flow of the conversation, gently pushed the paper with my new responsibilities back across the table, and politely broke the news that it was time for me to leave. The mission field was calling, and Beth and I had to obey. I never mentioned that the Lord had come into my room. I would never use a visitation from the Lord in an improper way. Visitations are holy and to be cherished. They have their purpose, and we need to be very careful that we don't use them beyond what they were intended for. This honors the Lord and keeps the door open for Him to trust us.

Transition in the kingdom of God can be very tense. When people have worked together for many years and have seen the Lord do so many wonderful things, and then one of them suddenly says, "It's time for me to go," can be difficult on many levels. It must have been such an experience for Elisha when he was separated from his master, Elijah, by a flaming chariot. Even though he knew it was the will of the Lord it still must have been a very emotional moment (2 Kings 2:12).

When I left the office that day, I was both excited and a little fearful about my future. Forty-eight hours after handing in my resignation, God sent a sign from

Asia, which came in the form of a letter from Bhutan. I was so filled with hope as I held that letter. Talk about encouragement!

The previous year, while working in India, I had met a Christian brother from the Himalayan kingdom of Bhutan. We were supposed to keep in touch, but I had not heard from him, so his letter came as a complete surprise. It was a handwritten note that simply said, "Brother Eric, are you coming to Bhutan?" With that letter in hand, I knew that we had made the right decision to transition toward overseas missions and that the Lord was ordering our steps.

JESUS SAID, "SO IS THE
KINGDOM OF GOD, AS IF A
MAN SHOULD CAST SEED
INTO THE GROUND"
MARK 4:26

CHAPTER 2

STEPPING BACK IN TIME

During the summer of 1995, before ever traveling to Asia, the Holy Spirit stirred us about praying for Bhutan. It was in our little living room, on Friday nights, where the youth would come to our Discipleship Training School in order to worship, pray, and be trained. Part of their curriculum was to focus on a nation or a region of the world and then strategize on how to reach it with the gospel. The year prior to this an evangelist had come to our church for a week of revival meetings. The power of God flooded the church and many lives were changed. More important, that joyful glory remained on our youth ministry after the evangelist left.

The meetings in our home were so filled with the Spirit of God that it was not unusual for kids to be overwhelmed by the power of God. It was also very common for youth to be stuck to the floor for long periods of time. I remember one particular Friday night when the meeting ended and parents arrived to collect their youth. One dad, leaving his car parked on the road, still running with the windshield wipers working, came into our living room looking for his son. Kids were worshiping and praying and many were on their faces before the Lord. I was leaning against the fireplace just watching the Lord move upon the youth when I glanced over to where the father had been, but he was gone. Where had he gone? I peered behind the sofa and saw that he had slid down the wall under the weight of the glory of the Lord and he too was stuck on the floor. I don't know what my neighbors thought when they saw kids leave my house like drunken teenagers, but after all it was Friday night! We were not drunk as you suppose, but abundantly filled with the Holy Ghost (Acts 2:15).

It was after one of these Holy Ghost youth meetings that Beth and I were led to pray over a map of the world. As we focused on the Himalayan region, we came across a country called Bhutan. That night we committed ourselves to fervently pray for that nation. At that time, there wasn't adequate information about that small, hidden Himalayan kingdom, but we got our hands on everything we could. Because of the lack of information, we found ourselves relying on praying in the Holy Spirit for Bhutan. It was during this time, as I mentioned earlier, that my pastor sent me to South India, via London Heathrow, to set up an evangelistic meeting there.

It was on my first trip to India that I had the long layover in London. As God was planting new direction in my spirit for Britain, He also was opening a door for me into Asia. This new door into the East opened for me one morning in Bangalore, India, while staying in the home of a missionary from our church.

On this particular morning I was upstairs praying when I heard the doorbell ring. When the bell rang, the Holy Spirit spoke very clearly: "Go downstairs." As I walked into the room, my missionary friend said to me, "These men are from Bhutan." When he spoke those words, I was filled with the Holy Ghost. I had never met or seen someone from Bhutan, and in this case, they were standing right in front of me. There, before my eyes, were two people that I had been praying for.

Bhutan, though a neighbor to India, was still four days by train from Bangalore. The missionary I was staying with had met the two men at the market earlier that morning. They had come to attend an Evangelism Explosion conference in South India which had been canceled, unbeknownst to them. However, their trip was not in vain; they met me instead, a man who was praying for Bhutan.

After talking for a while, we finally said our goodbyes and then closed with prayer. As we prayed together, the power of God fell on us. I was so overwhelmed and didn't know what to do except to give them an offering and a note with my address on it. When Simon, one of the Bhutanese evangelists, and his friend said goodbye, I had no idea if I would ever hear from them again.

Resuming the Story

A year later back in Richmond, I was standing with Simon's letter in hand, assured that God was ordering our steps. With this new confidence, I requested a meeting with my pastor so that I could share my vision with him.

Upon explaining my vision about moving to the UK, I realized his own frustration on how things were not moving forward as planned concerning the church's ministry base in London. The missionaries coming from Russia had not been granted entrance visas for the UK. Therefore, I thought that maybe my pastor would use the church's UK legal status to offer us an invitation. I soon found out that door was closed. Because the missionary couple had been denied legal entrance into the UK, I assessed that my pastor didn't feel comfortable taking the same approach with us.

Looking back, I can see that the Lord did not allow us to lean upon the things that were familiar to us. The Lord wanted to keep our dependency rooted in His ability. We were walking a path that we had never been on and had never seen before, and we were learning to trust Him for each step. This ensures that His plans and purposes come to pass correctly. Many times when receiving a vision from the Lord, we are tempted to run forward to accomplish it without really waiting on the one who gave it to us. The Lord loves to give vision, but He really loves it when we depend on Him for the steps needed to work it out.

One thing I will stress in this book is that the Lord wants to walk with us in fellowship so that everything done becomes a part of our relationship with Him. The Lord doesn't need us to do something for Him per se. He anoints us so that we can walk with Him. In this we find friendship with God and a fullness of life that is able to carry us through all the challenges that lie before us.

EXCEPT A SEED OF WHEAT
FALL INTO THE GROUND
AND DIES, IT ABIDES ALONE:
BUT IF IT DIES, IT BRINGS
FORTH MUCH FRUIT.
JOHN 12:24

CHAPTER 3

THE PLANTING

So much was happening in our hearts concerning direction. Our focus was now Bhutan with a strong stirring in our hearts to move to England. Both of these endeavors were rather expensive and demanded faith. The major challenge before us was how to legally establish our ministry base in the UK. Then the Lord stepped in and gave us wisdom on how to take the next step.

I have found that as believers move forward in the will of the Lord that He really does store up wisdom on behalf of the righteous (Proverbs 2:7). In this next step of direction we left Virginia and moved back to my hometown in Ohio to set up a legal charity in America. Then, from Ohio, our plan was to launch out to Great Britain.

Moving back to Ohio was easy for me. We were moving back to my parent's farm where I had grown up. It was there as a teenager where I learned to sit under the stars and meet with God. It was in those fields that my mother interceded for me pertaining to my calling to serve the Lord in ministry, as well as petitioning the Lord to send me to Oral Roberts University. As a result, it was in those same fields that the Lord's power came down upon me dramatically, healing me and then speaking to my heart about serving Him. I looked forward to returning to Ohio. For me, the family farm was a place of meeting with God.

We were now learning the patience of faith as we continued to seek a way to legally enter Britain. It was during this time of waiting that I began traveling to Russia to minister there. Russia, formerly known as the USSR, had now been open for the gospel for about six years and churches were being planted across that vast nation.

God's Plan is Like a Woven Tapestry

As I stated earlier, God's plan for our lives requires His leadership. As we yield to the Master Designer, He is able to impart into us that which unfolds and becomes a beautiful tapestry that carries the mark of the artistry of God. It is in this beautiful tapestry that we are able to look back and see the footsteps of God in the earth traveled through the frailness of our own feet.

My affinity to Russia and the Slavic nations began

as a child when my parents would travel into the former Soviet Union taking Bibles to the Russian believers. I loved to hear my parents' stories, especially of my father's experiences with the KGB. Their trips became the seeds of destiny in my own heart. My first trip into the former Soviet Union happened while I was a college student at Oral Roberts University.

I so loved ORU. It was a school that taught us about the power of the Holy Spirit and then afforded us the opportunity to do ministry on the weekends and foreign mission trips during our summer breaks. In June 1988, after completing my freshmen year, I went on my first summer mission trip to Nigeria. We saw people saved and healed, and I even got an opportunity to experience malaria! It was a true mission's experience. Our team was given the opportunity to work with the great apostle Benson Idahosa and his church networks around the nation. It was such an amazing experience to meet him and to eat at his table.

When I returned from Africa, my parents greeted me at the airport. I hugged my mother and she looked at me and said, "Keep your bags packed; you're heading to the Soviet Union with your father." It was on that particular trip, while taking hundreds of Russian Bibles to Christians in that far away land, that the Lord impacted my life very deeply.

Leningrad, Russia 1988

Flying into Leningrad (now known as Saint Petersburg) was quite an experience for me. Before we landed, while still in the air on our final approach, I could sense a strong spirit of control confronting us. Knowing that our suitcases were full of Bibles, which was technically forbidden, I couldn't help becoming extremely concerned. After landing and collecting our suitcases, we lined up and waited to cross the border. I was really nervous as I stood watching the border guards process the people ahead of us. My stomach seemed to be in a tight ball, and a slight bead of sweat began to form on my brow. Now it was our turn to approach the border agent. Sure enough, they found our Bibles and detained us. It was evident that they were not pleased with our desire to bring the gift of God's Word into the USSR. But seasons were changing for Soviet nations in the realm of the spirit, and God had placed us there on the forefront of watching it happen.

The year 1988 was special for the Russian Orthodox Church—it was the one thousandth anniversary of the Christian baptism of Kievan Rus. Technically, it was the time when Russia and Ukraine were united by faith. Even though those two nations, at the time of my trip, were firmly under the control of Soviet atheism, the government decided to recognize the anniversary as an important historical and religious celebration. It was also during this time that Prime Minister Mikhail Gorbachev was relaxing the government's control over the citizenry. Because of these two factors, we trusted God for a miracle of favor.

The shift officer then proceeded to question my father: "Why did you bring Bibles to the Soviet Union?"

My father innocently responded, "They are gifts; there is no harm intended."

The officer sternly retorted, "We will determine the harm!"

Just when all hope of getting through seemed lost, a higher-ranking supervisor walked into the room and questioned what was going on. The officer explained what had happened, and when the supervisor assessed the situation, he responded, "Because it's their [Christian] holiday, give them back their Bibles, and let them go." We stuffed the Bibles back into our bags and quickly left, while praising the Lord under our breath.

Two days after this miraculous intervention at the airport, our team of Bible-carrying American Christians visited the beautiful Leningrad Baptist Church. At that time, it was one of the only Protestant churches open for Westerners to visit in the USSR. Attending that service left an eternal mark in my heart. There in the balcony, as I watched the church service transpire, I noticed an older man on the ground floor sleeping and beginning to snore. His sleep was abruptly halted by a *"babushka"* (grandmother), who got up from her seat, walked down the row, and slapped him back into attention. I chuckled silently. I had grown up in church and had never seen such a thing in my life. As I sat reading my little travel New Testament, a Russian "grandmother" next to me looked intently at my Bible. When she caught my attention, she then reached into her carry bag and took out her "Bible"— it was pages of paper on which she had written out passages of scripture. That was all she had for a Bible.

I then motioned to my brother, who was sitting on the opposite end of the row, to give me a Bible from his bag. Excitement filled my heart as the Bible made its way to me. When it was in my hands, I handed her the full-sized Russian Bible, and she began to weep and say, "Spaciba, spaciba, spaciba" (thank you, thank you, thank you). I saw face-to-face what true hunger and appreciation for the Word of God was like. Sitting together with that little elderly Russian believer, we both were overwhelmed with tears of joy in the presence of the Lord. I realized why the Lord intervened at the airport and miraculously released our Bibles back into our hands. As our bus pulled away from the church that day, Russian believers chased after us with their hands in the air hoping to receive a Bible. I will never forget that picture. It reinforced in me the need that all nations have for the incorruptible seed of the Word of God. We had been sent to plant the Word of God, through Bible distribution, into the spiritual soil of that great nation.

My next trip into the Soviet Union as an Oral Roberts University student happened in 1990 on the eve of the Iron Curtain coming down. Our team traveled first to Finland to work evangelistically on the streets of Tampere. From Tampere, we stopped in Helsinki to pick up a shipment of Bibles and other Christian literature that we were to carry with us to Kiev, the capital of the Ukraine. There again, the Ukraine was still part of the Soviet Union, but the season in that area of the world had changed, and we were carrying much-needed gospel seed to plant into the soil of that nation "for such a time as this" (Esther 4:14).

We were based in Kiev with a group called New Life, which was focused on Bible and Christian literature distribution. The leaders of this organization were on the cutting edge of getting the gospel into their nation, and they opened the door for us to preach openly all over Kiev. We preached on the streets, sang, and performed dramas. We visited nursing homes, hospitals, youth clubs, movie studios, and schools. We did the unthinkable—we were a foreign group preaching Christ openly in the Soviet Union. We were on the forefront of a move of God in that region of the world. I vividly remember standing in Kiev's October Revolution Square doing many outreaches.

To the right of us was a giant statue of Lenin and surrounding us were crowds of people listening. On one particular outreach, it rained as we preached and sang, but the crowd didn't move. They just stood there, getting wet, while listening intently. Then, over the statue of Lenin, a beautiful rainbow appeared. Truly, the gospel is the hope of all nations.

While we preached on one side of the square, Ukrainian nationalists stood on the far side, protesting Moscow and urging people to join a nationalist movement. Ukrainians wanted to be free. I was greatly concerned by this knowing the strength of Soviet control and the years of oppression against anything that challenged the central powers. Also, I had been in Beijing, China, the year before (1989) with an Oral Roberts University mission team, where I witnessed firsthand the ruthlessness of Communist power.

Stepping Back to China

The year prior to being in Ukraine I was sent to China to teach university students English and to share the gospel. During that time, students across China had risen up to protest the central government. Located in the middle of Beijing is the great Tiananmen Square, standing as a gigantic monument to the vast strength of the Chinese people. It was in this massive square, which embodies the might of

China mixed with the pride of kings and dictators, both past and present, that the student movement made its home. This student rebellion had caught the world's attention, and the Chinese authorities were becoming very uneasy with what was happening.

Before leaving the capital to take up our summer teaching post in northern China, our team was given the opportunity to walk through Tiananmen Square. I remember the feeling of awe I experienced when I first stepped into that great square and beheld its immensity. I had been in Moscow's famous Red Square, but compared to Tiananmen, I had never been in such a vast place. Then we saw the students fortified against a monument in the center of the square. I still remember their faces. I will never forget their haunting questions: "Does America support us?" "Does America know what we are doing?" They knew that they had crossed lines and they wanted to know if the world would come to their rescue.

The Tiananmen Square Massacre

Five days later at our university in Northern China, via short-wave radio, we heard that the army had been sent to Beijing to end the protest. The students were massacred, arrests were made, and all others in the student movement were scattered. Because the students at our school did not have access to short-wave radio, they knew nothing of what had transpired in Tiananmen Square.

It had been only a few days earlier, upon arriving at our university, that our team of friendship evangelists began putting our lesson plans together while being formally introduced to our students. We knew that through building a bridge of relationship we would be able to share Christ with them. Obviously our plans were shattered by the military crackdown in Beijing and now we had to focus on our students in a more sobering way.

It took almost four days for the truth of what had happened to reach our city in the north. When it did, it caused major demonstrations all over the city. The students from the universities in our region were angry and they weren't backing down. Many of our own students had traveled back and forth to Beijing to be a part of the protests, and now the only thing they could do to vent their anger was to march. I remember the day when that changed. News had reached our school that the police and security forces were coming to search and arrest every student who had taken part in the protests. One morning I observed students, carrying makeshift bags that had been quickly fastened together, fleeing before the authorities arrived. The only students remaining at the university were students from Beijing who could not return home because of what was happening there.

Hot Spots in the Plan of God

Our team had been strategically positioned in a hot spot on the world stage for a God purpose. For the next few days it looked like China could potentially enter into a civil war. It was in those days after the massacre that the Lord opened a door of witness to our students. Many of them sat and wept, knowing that many of their friends and acquaintances had either died or been arrested. "Why did our government do this to us?" they asked with tears streaming down their faces. It was in closed-door meetings with our students that we shared Christ with them and then prayed for them and with them. They wanted freedom and now God was offering true freedom—a freedom that no Communist government could ever take away. We had been a seed planted into the soil of China for such a time as this.

At that time in China there wasn't an internet or Skype phone calls. We had to call a Chinese operator and request a call to the US. For some reason, I was the only one on our team who was able to get through to the USA. When I talked to my parents to assure them that I was safe, they relayed an urgent message from our school's administration: "Get out of China!"

We found one flight from the local airport that had the exact number of seats needed for our team. The morning we left for our next assignment in Hong Kong was the day the security forces arrived. As we pulled out to drive to the airport we watched police entering dormitories. The Chinese government had lost face in the eyes of the world, and now it was time to purge this problem, once and for all. Driving away, sensing the controlling power of the Communist government bearing down, we knew that we most likely would never see those students again. As Americans, we have no idea of the wonderful blessing of freedom we have and the price that has been paid to keep it.

Standing in a Different Square

Consequently, one year later in the USSR, standing in the October Revolution Square in the center of Kiev, I was concerned about a potential Soviet military crackdown. Thank God the crackdown never came. We were free to preach—and preach we did! It was during those years as a university student that God planted His love for the nations in me.

THY WAY IS IN THE SEA, AND
THY PATH IN THE GREAT
WATERS, AND THY
FOOTSTEPS ARE NOT KNOWN.
PSALMS 77:19

CHAPTER 4

GOD PARTS THE ATLANTIC

Though the Lord called us to position ourselves in Britain, Eastern Europe was important to me and I knew that I had to keep ministering in that region. As we waited for the legal door to open for Britain, I continued ministering on short-term mission trips to Russia. I knew that God would honor our faith and direct our steps. It was on such a trip in 1997 while flying back to America from Saint Petersburg, Russia, that God ordered my steps with His steps. During that flight home I had an overnight stop at Gatwick Airport, just south of London, next to the town of Crawley. As the plane circled the countryside, I stared out the window and thought how beautiful it was. In the quietness of my thoughts the Lord spoke to me: "A seed of righteousness, the planting of the Lord."

The joy of the Lord so filled me, even though I had no idea what that prophetic word meant. Upon landing I then traveled to my hotel, which was located in Maidenbower, a small village bordering Crawley. After arriving at the hotel and putting my bags in my room, I quickly went outside. As I walked around the community, I was so filled with joy. I thought, *I could move here.* Then the thought came to me, *How will we legally enter the UK?*

Many times when the Lord speaks a word to us, even though we are overwhelmed with joy, we often don't fully understand what it means. Upon returning home, I focused my faith in prayer toward the need of a legal door opening in Britain. One night while reading my Bible, I came across the passage in 2 Kings 13:14-19 where Elisha rebukes the king for weakly tapping the arrow three times. God had given the king a prophetic word of deliverance, but the king was lax in desire and thanksgiving as it pertained to God's promise of total victory. That night, I took the "arrow of faith" into my prayer closet. As I prayed for England, I struck the arrow repeatedly as an act of complete dependence on the Lord and as an act of faith declaring my intense desire for the thing required.

I will never forget the day when the phone rang as I sat in my parent's family room. My mother answered, and a man with a strong accent asked to speak to me. She quickly handed me the phone. It was the great revivalist Ashley Schmierer from Brighton, England. Ashley, an Australian farmer turned revival healing evangelist, had denominational oversight over all the Christian Outreach Centers in the UK. We had met on an earlier occasion, and in the course of our conversation, I had mentioned my need for a legal invitation to come to Britain. Ashley had felt the need to call and ask me if I still wanted to come to the UK. I was overwhelmed with joy. Of course I said yes! Upon hanging up the phone, I yelled to Beth, "Pack your bags! We're going to England!" What seemed like a huge impossibility was now completely made possible. God had gone before us, making the crooked places straight (Isaiah 45:1-3).

Now was the time to pack and prepare to ship all our earthly possessions to Europe. We were leaving house, lands, and family to go and serve the Lord overseas. At the time, it was a big step of faith for us. The verse from Psalm 139:9-10 kept coming to me: "Even across the sea, I will be with you!" As we approached our final departure date, I contacted a pastor in Columbus, Ohio, and asked if he would pray a blessing over us before we left the USA. I understood the importance of corporate faith in prayer before launching out as new missionaries to England.

On March 1, 1998, we were packed and ready to leave for Britain. Our household goods were already on a boat heading across the Atlantic, and now Beth and I were going to church to be prayed for. As we drove there we sensed a spirit of destiny already coming upon us, as if we were being immersed into a river of God's presence. That night when praise and worship finished, the pastor called us forward. When he placed his hands on us the power of God came upon us so mightily. I had never experienced such weight of glory. It took us several minutes before we could actually walk back to our seats. Something from heaven had been added to us and I will always cherish that moment. It was during that time of prayer that we were marked with these words: "You shall build a road of salvation from the south of England to Liverpool, and many shall walk upon that road." As we drove home that night I didn't know what to think—except I couldn't wait to get to England.

Arriving on English Soil

On arriving in Europe, I definitely had my own thoughts pertaining to God's plan for us in England. Looking back, I understood why such glory filled us before leaving America. We had no idea of the challenges that lay before us— challenges that would strip us of our own plans in order to keep us dependent upon God's plan.

Beth and I and our two small children moved to Hove, England, on March 3, 1998. Hove is a coastal town approximately fifty miles south of London. This little town is twinned with the city of Brighton. Both towns are geographically spectacular, with the English Channel to the south and the beautiful South Downs (rolling, lush green hills) to the north.

Brighton also is the beginning of the beautiful white cliffs that range along the south coast of England eastward toward Dover. It was those same white cliffs that gave the fliers during the Second World War such hope as they returned home from dangerous missions on the continent. The negative attribute was that both towns carried a strong demonic operation of witchcraft and perversion. It was a spiritual darkness that I had never encountered as a farm boy from Ohio, growing up in America. Once landing on the shores of Great Britain, we came into a head-to-head spiritual conflict out of which only the Lord could deliver us.

God Needs Seed

God needed a seed for Europe. And as the way of sowing and reaping goes, the seed must die before it can live and bear fruit. The presence of God that so filled us before leaving for Britain became the challenge to the spiritual atmosphere of those two coastal towns, and we were sandwiched somewhere between it all.

We had arrived with great expectancy of missionary ministry only to find that everything seemed to come to a halt. I had never experienced such intensity in spiritual warfare. Paul wrote to the Corinthians about this type of spiritual opposition.

*For we would not, brethren, have you
ignorant of our trouble which came to
us in Asia, that we were pressed out
of measure, above strength, insomuch
that we despaired even of life: But we
had the sentence of death in ourselves,
that we should not trust in ourselves,
but in God which raiseth the dead.*

2 Corinthians 1:8-9 KJV

Most Christians desire a scriptural life—except for the scripture just quoted! When I worked for the church in Richmond, I had known only a sense of success in ministry. Obviously, I wasn't living in America anymore; I was living in Europe, and all of the success I had known in ministry seemed to be vanishing before my eyes.

During that first year in Hove, an older couple came to our home and said that they had received a vision from the Lord for us. They explained that in the vision they had seen a giant, like a Goliath, that had risen up against us; for a season, it seemed like it would not move. Then they saw a wind of God come and strike it, causing it to crumble to the ground. I received that as a word of encouragement from the Lord, even though I had no idea when that "needed wind" would come and destroy the wall.

At the time I was traveling back and forth to India,

where we had established an outreach base and orphanage on the border of Bhutan. It seemed that was the only open door of ministry for us. I would travel to India and minister with such freedom, only to return to the UK, where there was such a sense of dread. It was beginning to look like we had missed God by coming to Britain.

If I have learned one truth about ministry, it is that when you are in the will of God, there will come a point when you question it. Remember, John the Baptist was a great prophet and forerunner of Christ Himself, but even he reached a point in the will of God when he was tempted to question Jesus. Was Jesus angry with John? No, and a thousand times no! Jesus graciously spoke words to remind John of who He was and He will do the same with us. Jesus is very kind and very gentle and He promised to be with us in order to complete what He has begun in us. He will never forsake us (Matthew 28:20).

As the year progressed, I felt a greater pressure of spiritual attack, and it seemed I wasn't able to break through it. One day, while driving north to London, I pulled off from the motorway near Crawley. (Yes, the same Crawley where I had spent the night en route home from Russia.) I felt such joy and peace as I drove around that area. For several months I had noticed that every time I drove near Crawley, joy would rise up in me. On the other hand, as I drove closer to Hove, I would sense a greater level of hatred against me. I was a new full-time missionary, far from home and family, in an all-out spiritual conflict on the mission field.

I had been sent to England to birth a ministry that I had never seen, and the spiritual opposition to the birthing process was very intense. One side note—even though we were locked into an intense spiritual conflict, our home was always full of peace. Friends and family would visit and comment on how peaceful our house was. That peace was there to minister to us as we continued to push through the darkness that was arrayed against us. The Lord, our Great Shepherd, is always faithful to make us lie down in green pastures (Psalm 23).

Making Adjustments

A change took place in our thinking concerning our location. I was new to the UK, and my thoughts were only about Hove, the south coast of England, and the wonderful church that had given us the legal invitation to Britain. At the time, I hardly knew that there was more to England than just the south coast. It seems like a crazy thought, but the intense warfare, as well as being a new missionary, worked together to close down my thinking. I knew in my heart that if we were going to survive on the mission field, we would have to change locations. It was time to get off Brighton's rocky beach and move inland. Even though the distance from Brighton to Crawley is only about thirty miles, in England that is not considered close and it's almost another world.

Normandy's Bloody Beaches

In June 1999, I sensed the Lord leading me to study D-Day, otherwise known as the Allied invasion of Normandy during World War II. While watching the famous John Wayne movie *The Longest Day,* a scene caught my attention that I will never forget. As the Allied landing craft approached the heavily fortified beaches of Normandy, young soldiers began readying themselves for an event that was far beyond anything for which they had trained. As they approached Normandy's cold coastline, some men prayed, while others began vomiting, and others kept talking, hoping to drown out their fears. Some knew by an inner knowing that they would not be going home, but they still chose to go forward in the cause. Regardless of what they understood about the day that lay before them, they were destined to become the seeds of liberty about to be planted into the darkness of European soil.

When the landing craft hit the beaches and the doors opened, such horrific fury broke loose. Many units suffered 99% casualties as they attempted to storm the beach. For those men who actually made it to the beach, they knew that the only way to survive the day was to keep moving forward. Fear would resign a man to stay on the beach where death's appetite was far from being quenched. Only raw courage would drive a man forward in order to live. I truly believe that survival was the first objective for the men landing on the beaches that day. It was raw, it was ugly, but out of the midst of it came what seemed impossible: victory!

Just as it was on D-Day, so it is in the realm of the spirit. There are wars, fierce wars that are arrayed against the servants of the Lord, who launch out to foreign lands. Sometimes the fierceness of these battles is designed to strip the Christian laborer of the hope to survive and carry on. Paul talks about such battles in his New Testament writings. In fact, the Holy Spirit anointed Paul to write many things about these conflicts. Satan knows that his time is short and he is filled with rage. That June in particular, I felt like the attacks and the pressure seemed too much for me to handle. It seemed as if we were dying in the soil of foreign missions in a land called Great Britain. The only thing I knew to do was to keep moving forward, by faith, even when I wasn't sure if my faith was working.

One night I told Beth that I needed to go for a drive and pray. I find that when I drive and pray I can be a little more free and loud. Driving north, while praying in the Holy Spirit, I found myself back in Maidenbower. Relieved at sensing a new-found peace,

I parked my car and prayed for about an hour. By now it was around midnight and I called Beth and told her that I wasn't coming home that night. I had prayed through to peace and refused to return to the battle. That night I slept in my car in a parking lot next to the community football (soccer) fields.

The Winch Principle

As the peace of God ministered to me, I made the decision to move out of Hove and up to Crawley. For a new missionary this was a big step. What was I going to do in Crawley? The wonderful church that had invited me to the UK had planted churches in many other cities, but not in Crawley. There seemed to be only one answer for us: move to Crawley and plant a church. Whether planting a church was right or wrong, I had to do something to start manifesting my gift and the anointing upon it so I could live and not die on the mission field. I also understood that sometimes in life you can seemingly lose your way and become stuck in a rut. On the farm we understood about being stuck in ruts. This is where the "winch principle"(as I call it) comes in. There are times when you need to take hold of something just off of your path in order to pull yourself out of the rut. Once out, then you correct yourself and keep moving forward. The church plant in Maidenbower was where I learned this principle.

On the night of our special ordination, the night

before leaving for the UK, our pastor spoke by the Spirit of God, warning us, "You are an evangelist. Don't be pulled into other callings when you get over there." Though I had not forgotten those words, it didn't matter. I felt hopelessly stuck, and I had to get out. The only way out was to start whirling my mantle, as Elijah had when he crossed the Jordan on dry ground. The life of faith isn't always pretty, but in the end, it is the only way of life on the earth that pleases God. When we boldly refuse to quit in the face of seemingly impossible situations, our heavenly Father and all of heaven tune in to the battle. I believe that is what Paul was talking about concerning being surrounded by a great cloud of witnesses (Hebrews 12:1). The devil hates tenacious faith because it causes heaven to draw close and surround you so that your faith will not fail.

So we moved to the Maidenbower- Crawley area! Then I booked a hotel conference room for Sunday meetings, and I walked and prayed over the houses in the area. There were times, as I walked through Maidenbower, when a spirit of prophecy would come upon me. As I prophesied, I would sense such a release of the Spirit of God concerning establishing a church in that community. In my heart of hearts, however, I wasn't satisfied with the idea of pastoring a church in England. The word of the Lord was to be an evangelist, not a pastor or a church planter.

Seed Requires the Correct Soil

In our move to Crawley, two things happened that positioned our steps toward our destiny. First, I had heard of an apostle to the British charismatic renewal. He was a mature man, and he was very English. The wonderful church that had originally invited us to the UK was Australian. As an American, I needed an Englishman to assist me in adapting to British culture. I remember our first meeting, when we sat down with Pastor Colin Urquhart in order to honor him and to respectfully explain that we were starting a church in Maidenbower. He just sat and listened and then smiled. He was rather quiet, yet loving and deep. That meeting has always stayed with me, and I will always cherish my other meetings with him.

The second thing that happened was that I heard about an asylum center located at Gatwick Airport, just a few miles up the road from Crawley. The asylum center was a detention facility for illegal aliens who had been arrested and were being held until their cases could be heard by an immigration court. After being apprehended, most of these people eventually were sent back to their nations. Upon hearing of this facility, my heart was drawn to make contact with the chaplain in order to request a ministerial position. Both of these meetings were doors that opened for us, and our ministry began to move forward in the nation.

Beth and I and our two kids, Caleb and Kelsey, moved to Crawley and got to work. We established a church plant in Maidenbower, as well as ministering at Tinsley House, the asylum center. The detention center became such a well of life for me, personally. At that time, I was so beaten up spiritually from my south-coast experience that I needed the Lord's presence to bring healing and strength back to me. The Lord declared in Matthew 25:36 that when He was in prison, He was visited. Obviously, He was inferring that acts of compassion done to those in need were the same as an act done to Him. The Lord takes this personally. I knew from this passage that I needed to go to where the needy were located in order to minister to the Lord. I knew that by doing this, the Lord would, in turn, minister to me, infusing me with His life. In short, I needed to be ministering at Tinsley House, where the Lord was, in order to survive on the mission field.

Even though we had moved to the UK in March 1998, it seemed we had yet to see the purpose for which the Lord had called us to England. The spiritual pressure against us was still intense, but the difference between Crawley and Hove was that we now knew we were in the right place. For the first time, I saw light at the end of the dark forest in which we seemingly had been trapped since landing in Britain eighteen months earlier. Part of the frustration we had was in knowing that we were not pastors.

Finally, toward the end of 1999, Beth and I received a word of wisdom concerning our church plant. The word was painfully obvious: "If you are not a pastor, don't become one!" At that, we closed the church and returned to the USA for a two-month furlough in order to refocus our vision. On a positive note, six months after we discontinued our church plant, Pastor Colin's leadership team started a new church in Maidenbower that is still functioning today. I truly believe that our "prophetic labors" in that community were not in vain.

Another milestone that took place during our first year in Britain was the formation of our own UK charity. Through this charity I could legally invite our family to live and work in Britain. Therefore, we were no longer dependent on other people inviting us to the UK. We were now in control of our own legal invitations to Great Britain. What a tremendous feeling!

The New Millennium—Full Speed Ahead

On January 2, 2000, we arrived back in the UK. We had survived the potential cataclysmic effects of Y2K, refreshed and ready to go forward. The church plant was a thing of the last century, and now, standing in the doorway of a new millennium, we looked forward to what God had for us. As we prayed, the Lord spoke to us a very clear word. In fact, we both heard it at the same time: "Go to Kingdom Faith." Excited for this new direction, I made an appointment with Pastor Colin and asked him if we could come to his church. He received us lovingly.

During the course of that year, I entered into a process of change. As missionaries, we often think that we are being sent to a nation in order to change the people. I have found, however, that is the farthest from the truth. I have matured into realizing that God sends us to places in order to change us. When God sent Jeremiah to the potter's house, Jeremiah had to watch for a while before the Lord spoke. As we change, we are then able to help others change. I am a little bit leery of imbalances that can arise from certain aspects of strong faith-preaching that can leave the potential missionary or Christian worker thinking that everything has to happen now. Or that everything has to happen the way we want it to. Some people believe that if results don't happen "now", then there must be something wrong with the one who believes. Remember, Moses lived in the desert for forty years before the Lord poured His glory upon him. David lived in the wilderness for over a decade before he was king. These two examples would not be accepted in today's model of success-driven ministry. When the Lord spoke the words in the Garden of Eden, "Let us make a man," he wasn't talking just about Adam. The Lord was declaring His creative purpose for all men. God is the Eternal Potter who created man to carry His glory in a clay pot. In short, the Lord is working with us for an eternal purpose and not only an earthly one. That is why I believe that God doesn't make ministries but rather vessels—and vessels take time!

Kingdom Faith, Horsham

Pastor Colin Urquhart was an Anglican vicar who, in the early 1970s, fervently sought God along with his congregation in Luton, England. In those early days of the Charismatic Renewal in the UK, the presence of God descended upon that little Anglican church. God had come down with revival fires, and the canopy of His presence not only rested upon that congregation, but it flowed out to Europe as well. Years later, I found myself sitting under this apostle of British revival. Being in services with Pastor Colin was a tremendous blessing. We worshipped for hours, and then prophecy would flow from the worship, and then he would teach. It was in those special meetings of waiting on the Lord that I realized that God was changing me.

Two things happened during this season of change. First, Britain, the nation itself, was changing. The ministry of CrossWalk and FourSmiles would not have worked in an earlier season. Also, in order to intersect the change coming upon Europe, God had to change me. As I look back, I can see why I didn't have a clue what God wanted me to do when we originally left for Britain. In fact, I lost relationships because certain friends in America thought I was a failure. The problem was, they didn't understand the process of changing seasons upon nations and that God has to create vessels to carry the glory into those seasons.

The Lord was stripping me of the American mindset of success driven ministry that I had known and operated in while living and working in America. Though there was nothing technically wrong with this mindset, the reality was, I wasn't living in America anymore. We had moved to Britain, which is a completely different culture on a completely different continent. Faith always produces results, but the second greatest agent of success is patience. Faith must work with patience (Hebrews 10:36), and sometimes we get very uncomfortable at the amount of patience needed to produce the intended results. In this process of change, the Lord was teaching us to depend upon Him.

BEHOLD, THERE WENT OUT A
SOWER TO SOW
MARK 4:3

CHAPTER 5

GOD GIVES SEED TO THE SOWER

Writing the Smile Tract

Although many adjustments were made, and things were moving forward, we were still dissatisfied and wondered when we would begin the ministry for which the Lord had called us to Britain. There had been much praying, much weeping, and much change, but we were still not satisfied. One morning, after a wonderful time of prayer, I felt inspired to write a gospel evangelism tract (leaflet). I headed to my office, which was located in the stairwell of our house, and sat down at my computer and wrote the "Four Reasons Why You Can Smile" evangelism tract. I began with the ultimate truth: *God loves you!* I proceeded further with the revelation that *Jesus died for you.* Following these two powerhouse truths was the third reason to smile: *God has a good plan for your life*. Reason number four tied everything together: *Today is your day*, meaning that you need to make a decision now to receive the gift of God's grace. When I finished writing the Smile tract, I looked at it and wondered if I would ever use it. I wasn't even sure I liked it, and furthermore, in all outward appearances, I wasn't smiling. We were learning to live by faith on the mission field, and with that Spirit of faith, we were learning how to draw joy from the wells of salvation in our hearts (Isaiah 12:3). Simply put, I wrote the Smile tract by faith and joy, not by a natural sense of happiness. At times, the enemy's attacks were relentless, but we learned to shelter in the secret place of the Most High. Our presence in Britain was disturbing darkness and that darkness wanted us out of Britain.

After writing the Smile tract, I looked at it and thought that I would never use it. So I created a file and put it in the drawer. I continued to minister to those seeking asylum at Tinsley House, and because I went there faithfully, God granted me favor with the management. In fact, I had become a part of the chaplain's inner circle, which granted me security clearance to go and come without prior permission. God went before me, and He only needed me to follow. As the year came to an end, Beth and I were very frustrated with the whole British vision and purpose. We had been waiting upon the Lord and praying, and it still seemed that we had not fully entered into the purpose for which the Lord had sent us to Europe. Then the day came when I finally called it quits. I'd had enough of Britain and wanted to go home.

On that particular morning, I said to Beth, "I quit! We are leaving." All the prophetic words were more like pathetic words. We felt as if we'd missed God's will, and the only reasonable thing left for us was to return home—back to our culture, our people, and our nation. Even though I had made this decision in my head, something deep in my heart had not fully let go. There is something about prophetic purpose that doesn't turn loose so easily. In this state of mind, I called an airline and talked to them about one-way tickets to the USA. Then I called an international shipping company to arrange sending my household things back to Ohio. I remembered the joy and excitement I'd had when shipping all of our earthly belongings to Europe, and now the sense of failure was setting in as I made plans to ship them back. I had reached the end and I was going home—or at least I thought I was!

After a conversation with the airlines, I headed upstairs to our bedroom with a sense of great dismay. I turned my laptop on and opened the CD drive. When I pushed a CD down upon the drive, the drive itself broke. Under such stress, I must have pushed it too hard. When it broke, I became more depressed. I thought, *I can either fix it here in England or after I return to America.* I decided to fix it in England.

I called Toshiba UK and asked them about a repair center. They directed me to a company in the city of Reading. I phoned this company and spoke with a sweet older lady. She was so kind to me, which I found quite unusual. There was something about the way she spoke to me that captured my attention. She said things like, "Bless your heart." It was like I was talking to a person of prayer, and in an odd way, God was using her to minister to my heart.

By the time I hung up the phone, I really wasn't thinking about my laptop anymore. I was drawn by the love I'd felt from the phone call. I told Beth, "I need to drive to Reading to pray." At the time I didn't fully understand what was happening, but I did know that I sensed rays of hope.

From Crawley, I drove over an hour to Reading. As I drove around the city, while continuously praying in the Holy Spirit, I found myself in a little area called South Reading. I sensed a drawing to the area. While driving around the community, I found a sports facility called South Reading Leisure Centre. Then a joyful thought came to me: *"Would you come here, before you leave England, and tell these people that I love them?"*

I responded, "Yes, before I leave England, I will come and tell people that you love them." As I prepared to drive home from Reading I received a prompting to stop at a grocery store and ask for a copy of the Yellow Pages. I opened the phone book and found the page that listed local churches and places of worship; I ripped it out and took it home. Joy bubbled up—and I hadn't had joy like that for a long time.

The next day, I called churches in Reading. I explained that I was coming to Reading to tell people that Jesus loved them. When I asked if they would help me, one church after another answered no. Some had no interest, while others were skeptical or cautious about who I was. I felt such discouragement come back upon me. The last church I called was Zion Assembly of God. An older man answered the phone. I already had prepared myself for rejection, but the man never rejected me. I said, "My name is Eric Casto, and I am coming to Reading to tell people that Jesus loves them. Would you like to help?"

Surprisingly, the older pastor replied, "Yes".

I was shocked. I then said, "It's in two weeks!" I thought, *Surely he will reject me now.* Pastors typically need six months in order to prepare to reach people.

He responded, "Okay, that sounds good."

Then I thought, *Now for the real test.* I sheepishly declared, "I'm an American."

From the other end of the phone came his quizzical reply, "I know that!"

Planting the Heavens

I realized that we actually had a date, and I was filled with hope. The next day I discussed the opportunity with Pastor Colin, and he released several Bible school students to go with me. Then I did something that changed my ministry forever. I reached into the file cabinet and pulled out the "Four Reasons Why You Can Smile" tract to print it for the Reading outreach. I printed five hundred tracts on bright yellow paper for the outreach, while having no idea if they would even be received. I remembered the street outreach we did during the London Ablaze meetings, and I definitely had not forgotten the hardness we encountered on the streets of London. Little did I know that the bright-yellow smiling preacher was being readied to touch the nations of the earth, far reaching, beyond the city limits of Reading. I was stepping into the harvest fields of God, where the heavens would be planted with a seed of His Word and a Smile! (Isaiah 51:16)

The Smile tracts were printed and ready, and I was off to Reading. I will never forget walking into that little church and the shock I received. Eight people were waiting for me to arrive. One said, "We have been praying that God would send us someone to teach us evangelism." I briefly thought, *You obviously didn't pray hard enough: you only got me!*

That day we walked through South Reading, knocked on doors, gave out tracts, witnessed to people, and prayed with many of them. The Smile tracts were a great success. The day was saturated in joy, and I was filled with the presence of the Lord. The Lord was working through me while restoring life in me. While driving home that night from Reading, I thought, *I am now free to leave England.*

Then my phone rang. It was the chaplain of Tinsley House. He said, "Eric, Prince Charles is coming to the center for a royal visit next week, and we would like you to be a part of the clergical delegation to greet him." Of course I was elated! The thought of meeting Prince Charles before leaving the mission field helped soothe the thoughts of failure that were waging a war inside of me.

In the Shadow of the King
There is Favor

That morning as I arrived at Tinsley House, the center looked like a police convention. Security was everywhere, and I wasn't sure what I was in for. As management organized the crowd into smaller groups, I was somehow placed in the first group that would greet Charles when he entered the room. As we stood waiting, I was aware of the presence of God filling the room. Something was about to happen, and my spirit was so stirred. I can only describe the anointing that I experienced that day as a British anointing. The Bible is very clear that the Lord anoints men and women to lead nations. Whether they understand it or not, the royal family definitely has an anointing upon them for Great Britain. I had never sensed anything like it. (*To understand this further, I suggest watching the video of Queen Elizabeth II's coronation. There is a point where she pledges to defend the Christian faith, which then is consummated by her being anointed by the Archbishop of Canterbury in the "secret place." It is a very moving event to watch.*)

As I pondered what was happening in my heart, Prince Charles came through the door and walked over to greet us. As he spoke with us, the newspapers began taking pictures in order to capture the historic event. The immigration issue was—and still is—an important issue in Britain. The royal visit was to bring to the forefront the work of the UK's Home Office as pertaining to how asylum seekers were being treated in a humane and uplifting way. Though the center operated like a prison, those detained were free to leave at any time; that is, to return to their original countries. The chaplain and other ministers of religion were there because of the role we played in ministering to the spiritual needs of those detained. When Prince Charles and I shook hands, something went into me and unlocked a door in my heart for Britain. I don't understand it, but I do know it happened. The next day, my picture with Prince Charles was in several UK publications. Only God could have set that up! There is favor in the shadow of the king!

After meeting Prince Charles, I drove home wondering what was happening in me. I sat down in our living room feeling like I was on cloud fifteen, (forget cloud nine)! I said one simple prayer: "Lord, what is happening?" I remembered that I had quit two weeks before.

Then the word of the Lord came to me: "When you came to your end, you found my beginning!" Obviously, I didn't leave Britain but decided to stay. I looked at the map of England and targeted major British city centers. I mapped out a road from the south of England north to Liverpool. I saw a circuit of evangelism that needed to be plowed. I now understood the purpose for coming to Europe. The season had come and it was time to plow and to plant Britain with the Word of God.

With our move from Hove to Crawley, I'd found myself in the right place. Being in revival meetings with Pastor Colin helped us to adapt to England as well as to Europe. Finally, when I met Prince Charles, something was released for me to carry seed into the nation. I had received favor in order to move forward in ministry in Great Britain.

As I think back to the word the Lord spoke to me in 1997 when I flew over Crawley, declaring "a seed of righteousness," I finally understood the wisdom of God. Now, several years later, just under the place where the Lord spoke to me was the town where I wrote the Smile tract. Armed with seed, we launched out into the ministry of building a road of salvation from the south of England to Liverpool. As we went by faith, the warfare against us weakened. We also realized that there was much more to England than just the south coast. Truly, our steps were being ordered by the Lord.

AND I HAVE PUT MY WORDS
IN THY MOUTH, AND I HAVE
COVERED THEE IN THE
SHADOW OF MINE HAND,
THAT I MAY PLANT THE
HEAVENS.
ISAIAH 51:16

CHAPTER 6

THE BIRTH OF CROSSWALK AND FOURSMILES

The FourSmiles outreaches in the UK began in the city of Reading. One month later I was in Oxford and then off to Northampton. In these three cities our teams, supplied by Kingdom Faith Bible College, only passed out Smile tracts. Then the idea of building a cross came to me. People often ask me how I came up with the idea of carrying a cross. I almost don't know how to answer that question. I do know that I had a strong inward witness that I was supposed to do it. It was an impression that came upon me and ordered my thinking to get it done. I had never built a cross so I prayed about how to do it. I knew a man from our church named John Hutchinson. John was a skilled carpenter who knew how to build anything made of wood. I ordered the wood, and John built my cross. I found a company in the UK that sold cedar wood from the USA, so that both missionary and cross ended up originating from the same country. The cross was roughly 12 feet long and 4 inches by 4 inches thick. At the bottom of the cross we affixed a trailer jockey wheel so that I could easily walk with the cross and not end up dragging it. John built the cross in three sections so that it could easily be taken apart, then put into a special bag, and carried on airplanes. Before our family moved from England, John had built four additional crosses for various other evangelistic outreaches. I accused John of having Roman blood in him based upon the many crosses he built. John was a good man.

Sent to Coventry

In English culture the term "being sent to Coventry" can carry a negative connotation. For many, it would mean being rejected and treated as if invisible. For me, Coventry was where I began walking with the cross, and I definitely wasn't invisible! Because I was new to walking with the cross, it took me a little while to figure out how to walk under low-hanging signs. I remember walking down the sidewalk next to a major road when the top of the cross hit a road sign, almost causing me to stumble and fall over. People in cars laughed at me, which brought further revelation that if I carried the cross I would have to learn to be laughed at. My pride was being challenged.

Over the years, I have heard much laughing and

cursing directed at me. Because of the hatred and mocking that sometimes occurs, I have learned to abide in the secret place of God's love. In abiding, I have found grace in His calling upon me to walk with the cross. From the beginning of the actual CrossWalks, I heard a common phrase: "Jesus didn't have a wheel." This phrase is so common I hear it in every nation and language. I am almost sure it is a mocking spirit that comes upon people when they come near me and the cross.

In the beginning days of this type of ministry, I would rear up to respond to such foolish talk. As time has passed, however, I've grown in my ability to love these people and simply smile at them. It doesn't faze me anymore. There are times when God's love flows like a river around me, causing me to hold onto the cross to keep myself from falling over. There is a weight to the love of God. We only experience a measure of the tangible weight of that love here on the earth. Scripturally speaking, God's love has been poured out upon us, making us children of God, but we still have no earthly understanding of the true height, depth, length, and width of His love. I really believe that it will take an eternity for us to comprehend how great his love is for us.

As I minister in cities and villages, interacting with thousands upon thousands of people, my heart is deeply touched at how great the mercy of God is for all of us. His hands reached out and touched lepers, making them whole. His fingers brought hearing to the deaf. His beautiful arms held children while He spoke blessings over them. It must have been amazing to watch Jesus take bread and break it, and as it left His hands it began to multiply. Then the day came when those beautiful hands were freely given to Roman soldiers to pierce with nails. There was not one ounce of bitter hatred in Jesus. There was no defiance in His stare. Man's Creator made a way for love to come upon humanity and ultimately reside within man's heart. God, through the cross, was restoring man, through an operation of grace working by faith, unto His likeness. (Ephesians 2:8)

Though I walk with the cross, I cannot say that I fully understand the depth of God's love, because I don't! I do understand, though, why Paul prayed for the church to be strengthened with God's might, by the Holy Spirit, in the inner man or human spirit. (Ephesians 3:16-17). God's love is the greatest spiritual force in creation. The four living creatures around the throne of God, so close to the Creator, who is love, cry, "Holy, holy, holy." Therefore, the greatest characteristic of God, who is love, is found in the word *holy*. Therefore, it requires God's strength to walk in God's agape-love.

When God's love comes so strong at times, I will stop and hold on to the cross. Often a team member will see me and ask if I am tired or need a hand. In these special operations I am very aware that the voice of the Lord is speaking to the hearts of men and women. My part is to stand and let them look at the cross. Like the operation of a winnowing fork, the Holy Spirit removes the chaff around the hearts of those intently gazing in order to pave a way for their salvation. Many times people stare, caught up in God, but I never see them. At times, other people near to the cross become stuck and have no idea that they are not moving. Usually, once they receive a tract, they walk on. One thing I know is that it has nothing to do with me and everything to do with the love of the Lord. We definitely have a part in salvation, even though we cannot save. It is the voice of the Lord in the human heart that opens the door for their salvation.

In that first year of walking with the cross, I felt the spiritual attacks against us change. They were no longer directed in a way to keep us from moving forward. Now we were moving forward and accessing British city centers with a spirit of faith and the love of God. During that first year of CrossWalks, just before going into a new city, it was common for one of us to be spiritually attacked in our bodies or in our sleep. We learned to laugh at those attacks because we knew what they were. I also believe that all those years of waiting on the Lord produced a strength inside of us that enabled us to resist those fierce attacks.

Beautiful You Are to Me

At that time, a wonderful brother named Andy started to travel with me. Andy was an excellent guitarist and singer. We would walk into a city, and I would hold the cross and preach, and then Andy would sing a song he wrote called, "Beautiful You Are to Me". When he would sing, it was like the Holy Spirit was singing to the people and washing them in the love of God. On one particular Saturday we traveled to the city of Derby (pronounced Darby). Derby is in an area of the Midlands where the local people greet you by saying *me duck*. Hello, me duck! Put a strong, thick English accent on it, and you will have it.

Derby is a popular attraction for the ghost tourism industry in Britain. It is a town steeped in witchcraft and a craving to interact with the dead, especially with ghosts. I will never forget the day before going to Derby, when my mother called to inform me about a program she saw on TV. It was all about Derby and ghost walks. According to the television program, Derby was the ghost-walk capital of England. God was ordering my steps and providing me with information concerning what I would have to deal with in the spiritual atmosphere of that city. (*Though I mention one aspect of this city, it is by no means a judgment against it. There are many beautiful things about Derby as well. One of the greatest aspects of Derby is the people. If you ever travel into that area of England, you will definitely enjoy interacting with the locals.*)

We had a small team that Saturday that consisted of four adults and Andy's young daughter Jessica. As soon as we entered the city limits, we could sense the spiritual oppression greeting us. When I am in the CrossWalk and FourSmiles anointing, I become very sensitive to whatever is operating spiritually in a city. When the prophet Samuel came to Bethlehem to sacrifice unto the Lord, the authorities of the town came out to greet him. As the old prophet approached the city, the elders standing and shaking in the presence of the Lord would ask, "Why are you here?" This is a good picture of what happens with evangelistic ministry. As the Christian workers approach a city the devils become afraid. In order to protect their territory, they will meet you at the border of the city to intimidate you. The Lord instructed me in the beginning of this ministry that my attitude was to be like that of Samuel. My declaration is simple: "I have come to worship and sacrifice before the Lord, and it is none of the devil's business."

In the early days of CrossWalk, even though we had received our breakthrough, I still felt spiritually weak. It was amazing to see how things moved forward, but internally, I was still recovering from the intense spiritual warfare from our days living on the south coast. I felt like I was walking with a spiritual limp. What made CrossWalk work was my dependence on the Lord. It was during this time that I made a decision to never belittle or criticize what any man does for the Lord. When I walk with the cross, I always remember that the battle, at one time, was too much for me and that I had quit. In my quitting, I also remember how the Lord began, which causes me to love Him even more. In its simplest form, I walk with a cross as a way of loving the Lord and sacrificing before Him, which has nothing to do with the opinions of men or devils.

As we drove into Derby, Jessica suddenly began throwing up in the car. Andy put the window down and shoved her head out as she vomited all over a roundabout. Both angels and demons had to have had a laugh at what that looked like that day. We took authority over it in the name of Jesus, and it broke.

When we finally arrived and started ministering in the town, things went crazy. Maybe I should say that people went crazy. I have never seen so many people come under a demonic presence that energized them to challenge us in order to stop us. Thankfully, they could only come so far and then were stopped by an invisible wall.

Bright yellow smiles went out by the hundreds. As we passed out the Smile tracts, we gained a knowledge about which people we needed to spend more time with. We had gone forth with seed, and that seed was planted into the hearts of men and women.

Driving home from Derby, we knew we had won

the day. We had been working in the harvest fields of God, planting the seed of His kingdom, and we were full of joy.

London—the Epicenter of CrossWalks

By the time the year came to a close, I sensed I needed to do a London outreach. I was armed with Smile tracts and a cross, and now Britain's beautiful capital was in my sights. December 2001 was the first London CrossWalk at Christmas; it would eventually be known as the London CrossWalk in December. The outreach was five days long and was located in the heart of both the city of Westminster and the actual city of London. (*The city of London is the original city within the heart of what is known as "Metropolitan London". Today, the city of London is the center of banking and commerce and is also home to the magnificent Saint Paul's Cathedral.*)

Words cannot explain the feelings I had the first time I walked onto Westminster Bridge. With Big Ben before me, I saw thousands of people from all over the world, and they, of course, saw me. It was during that week, as I walked onto the bridge, that the power of the Lord came down upon me. Power, like liquid fire, shot down into my bones. Then the words came to me: "You walk, and I'll talk." I will never forget those words. With those words came knowledge that I was just as anointed to carry the cross as I was to hand out tracts. It also gave me an understanding that the voice of the Lord would be heard as I carried the cross. As that power came down upon me, I realized that I couldn't speak. All I could do was walk with the cross, while bright-yellow Smile tracts flowed out like a river. I could sense such love being poured out around us. The cross was cutting through the spiritual atmosphere on that bridge, where the nations of the world were walking.

By the last day of that week of CrossWalks, I realized that I had changed. Though I was tired physically, my spirit had been strengthened with might. Heading back to Westminster from Saint Paul's Cathedral that night, I slowed my pace as the team continued on before me. The sun had gone down several hours earlier, and a slight mist was in the air. Walking onto the Golden Jubilee Bridge across the Thames River, I observed a street cleaner at the far side coming toward me. The team was now a fair bit ahead of me, leaving the cleaner and me alone on that pedestrian bridge.

I then noticed that someone had dropped a Smile tract, and the cleaner was walking over to pick it up. As I slowly approached, I watched with anticipation to see what was going to happen next. It was dark, and the cleaner was standing under a street-light accented by a gentle mist in the air. It was a very magical moment. In some ways, it was like the closing scene of a movie. I then thought: *What is going to happen?*

Will he throw it into the bin, or will he keep it? It was like the efforts of the whole week would be summed up by what he was going to do with that tract.

The man picked up the tract and briefly read it. He then took his gloves off, gently folded the tract, and put it into his pocket. Then the word of the Lord came to me: "I have spoken to London this week, and many have heard My voice." Tears formed in my eyes. The week had been long and hard, and many spiritual atmospheres had been plowed by the cross. The furrows created by the plowing had also received thousands of gospel seeds (tracts). As we drove home from London, I couldn't help but realize that I had changed that week—in a good way. The first phase of CrossWalk had been completed. We had produced the Smile tract, built a cross, and plowed English city centers.

HE MAKES HIS ANGELS WINDS
AND HIS MINISTERS A FLAME
OF FIRE
HEBREWS 1:7

CHAPTER 7

SIGNS, WONDERS AND THE MINISTRY OF ANGELS

Behold, I send an Angel before thee, to keep thee in the way, and to bring thee into the place which I have prepared.

Exodus 23:20

Angels and Rush Hour

It was during our first year as missionaries when I traveled to London to purchase a piece of video equipment. My son Caleb, age five, and I boarded a train and traveled north into central London. When we arrived at Victoria Station, we exited the train and made our way to the underground metro, commonly known as the tube. Being a normal little boy, Caleb loved trains—which made this an exciting outing for him. Everything was going great. We arrived at Tottenham Court Road, purchased the equipment, and then headed back to the tube station. There was, however, one thing I hadn't anticipated, which was the time of day we chose to return home. It was now rush hour, and the tube was packed with people.

As I approached the platform, while pushing through crowds of people and trying to hold onto both Caleb and the bulky camera equipment, that my heart became afraid. Every parent panics at the thought of accidently being separated from their child in a massive crowd. Suddenly, I became extremely concerned with what could happen if we were separated. What would I do if I was pushed onto the train and Caleb got pushed off? At that moment I wasn't able to put the equipment down and hold on to him properly. As my heart began to fear, a very kind Englishman walked up to me and asked if he could help. I didn't think twice; I gave the stranger the camera equipment, I grabbed Caleb, and together, we jumped onto the tube.

After reaching Victoria Station, we all exited the tube and went upstairs to the train platforms. When we arrived at the platform, the man gently returned the camera equipment and asked if there was anything else he could do. I said, "No, but thank you very much." As Caleb and I walked toward our train, I turned around to look for the man, but he was gone. Then the Holy Spirit spoke to my heart: *"When you became afraid, I moved in that much closer."* You might ask if the man was an angel. I would probably say yes because of how the whole thing occurred and the help I received. But in the final analysis, the thing that mattered most is that we were helped.

In our teaching segments for CrossWalk, I usually talk about seeing the ministry of angels. In my walk with the Lord I have never asked to see angels, but rather that I would recognize their ministry on my behalf. This prayer does not put undue pressure on the Lord for a spiritual experience. Rather, it is a prayer that our eyes will be open to see the Word of God in operation around us. Angels are always in operation when the Word of God is declared and believed. I encourage CrossWalk teams to expect angelic ministry in our midst. Scripturally, I believe that this prayer is permissible to pray.

Pulled to the Cross

Over the years, I have witnessed some very interesting sights that only could be attributed to the ministry of angels. On my second outreach in Reading, a man walked up to me to take a Smile tract. What stood out was that his shirt sleeve was pulled out, as if someone had pinched it and was bringing him to me. Upon receiving the Smile tract, he corrected his course and went on his way.

Was I able to personally witness to him? No, I was

not a part of that man's thoughts. He was brought to me in order to receive a thought from the Lord. I truly believe Isaiah 65:1 where the Lord declares: "I am sought by those who asked not for Me, I am found by those who sought Me not!" The majority of people with whom I interact are not thinking about God, but God is thinking about them. Salvation never begins with man's thoughts. This ministry is anointed to initiate a new thought in people by planting a seed of the Word of God into their hearts. There have been many times over the years when I witnessed the operation of angels bringing people to me.

Wisdom Cries Out on the Streets
Proverbs 1:20-23

There is a difference between talking about the gospel and preaching the gospel. Both have tremendous purpose in witnessing. While preaching on the streets I will declare short power-packed truths that follow the outline of the Smile tract. After I preach for a while I will wait a minute or two, catch my breath, and then repeat it. This operation of street preaching plants the Word of God into the hearts of those who hear, as well as those who don't want to hear. Through faith-filled, loving declaration, God gets equal time for a few minutes in a person's life. Unfortunately, many people live in such a way that they become content in the comfort of their lives.

Many of these people are accustomed to listening to the devil whose lies dominate their thinking. Because of this God will move upon someone to preach for a few minutes on a street corner to break up the atmosphere in a person's heart. Though the sermon may seem short and small in comparison to everything else in that person's life, it still carries with it the dynamic of seed. A very small seed, the size of a mustard seed, has the power to move mountains in a person's life (Matthew 17:20). Never underestimate the eternal power of the incorruptible seed of the Word of God.

The Dog that Sat Down

On our second outreach in Derby, I had just started to preach when a man walking his dog entered the area where our team was passing out Smile tracts. He was adamant about not wanting our gospel leaflet. The man proceeded to go on his way. When I lifted my voice to preach, almost instantaneously, the dog sat down, as if he was listening to the sermon. The man tried and tried to move the dog, but he couldn't. After a few minutes, I paused, and when I did, the dog stood up and walked away. Obviously, this gave the dog's owner a sense of relief that he could finally leave. That's when I took a deep breath and continued preaching. The dog sat back down and his owner had to stand there and listen to the gospel. It was like an angel had come and placed his hand upon the dog's head and wouldn't release him until I had finished preaching. Sometimes animals have more sense than humans.

The Brick That Was Stopped in Mid-Air

In 2002, Europe experienced heavy rains that caused terrible flooding in various areas. Prague had been flooded, leaving much renovation to be done in the center of the city. On one particular outreach there, a man became angry when I began to preach. The Czech Smile tracts were going out so peacefully, but things always change when the preaching begins. I began to declare John 3:16 when a man took a flood renovation brick and threw it at me. The wonderful thing is that something or somebody stopped the brick in mid-air and threw it down. No one was hurt— especially me. Once again, thank God for angels.

The Frozen Daughter

As I was preaching the gospel on Regent Street, London, a father with his young daughter attempted to walk past me. When they were directly in front of me, the young girl froze and stared at me, listening intently. The father attempted to move her on, but he couldn't. Though the girl was around eight years old, she was totally immovable to the grown man. Not only did she stand still and listen to me, but so did her father and another man with them. How did that happen? It had to be an angel, putting his hand on the young girl's head and holding her there until they had received a seed of truth planted into their hearts. Remember, salvation does not begin with man, but rather with God, walking into the garden of men's lives and speaking a word to them. That family received a message from heaven that day.

Frozen at the Trash Can

The Et'hem Bey Mosque stands in the center of the Albanian capital of Tirana, where approximately 60 percent of the population is Muslim. It was late, and the street-lights came on while we were finishing our outreach near the mosque. As the bright-yellow seeds of the Smile tract went out, a lady walked by and took one, opened it, and kept walking. She read it and then promptly walked over to the trash bin and threw it away. As soon as the tract left her hand, she froze, standing still while staring into the waste bin. Then suddenly, she turned around, walked back, and asked for another gospel leaflet. She took it, put it into her purse, and walked off into the night.

The assistant pastor working with me got the biggest smile and look of wonder on his face. He said, "Did you see that? You could see God speak to her after she threw the tract away. It was as if the Lord stopped her and said, '*You need that!*'" It was very clear what had happened to her, even though we never heard a voice. Angels are sent to minister to those who will be heirs of salvation!

Three English Smile Tracts

Recently in Paris, I trained an outreach team from a local church to work with me. On this particular walk two other people joined me who had traveled from a city three hours away. I printed several thousand French tracts and was rather excited about walking and planting Paris with a smile. As of this writing France has been rocked by many terrible terrorist attacks. Several of these attacks focused on Paris. Because of this potential danger, central Paris was heavily fortified with soldiers who walked around with machine guns. On my first walk in Paris, the church assisting me was a little apprehensive about the possibility of the police stopping us. We had no permit to walk with the cross. I reassured them, "Don't fear. I really believe that God is with us and that France is in a new season."

Eventually, the police did stop us and asked what we were doing. Our response was simple: "We carry a message of love and hope for France."

They responded, "Keep up the good work!" God had granted us favor with the police.

On my second Paris CrossWalk, after ministering on the streets from City Hall toward the famous Bastille, the team asked if they could take a break for lunch and coffee. While the team went to eat, Bernadette and Jeremy, two team members who had driven three hours to be with us that day, stayed with me and continued to talk with people and hand out French Smile tracts. Interestingly, Jeremy, a new Christian, found three English tracts in his hand.

"Where did these come from?" he asked, while handing them to Bernadette, who then walked over to me with a puzzled look.

"Eric, where did the three English tracts come from?" she inquired.

As soon as she handed them to me, three Turkish Muslims walked up to us and stated, "We don't speak French!" Upon this declaration they kindly gave the French tracts back.

I immediately responded, "Wait—I have three English tracts that were just given to me. They are for you!" They took them, thanked me, and walked away.

I stood there with my mouth open and wondered what had just happened. Where had the three English tracts come from? Three people, three tracts—perfect timing. Only our God can do things like that! Though miraculous, those three Turkish Muslims had no desire to stand there and talk with me. But that didn't affect the Lord's desire to talk to them. This ministry is anointed to plant the gospel into the lives of those who, though they haven't asked yet, are seeking (Isaiah. 65:1). The kingdom of God is likened to a sower going forth to sow the Word of God (Mark 4:3).

Speaking to the Weather

England is known for rainy and overcast weather. While living in England we became quite used to rain, but like most people living there we never carried an umbrella. Drizzly rain was a part of life. With the CrossWalk, however, I began to notice weather changes as I went forward with the outreaches. When I was a student at Oral Roberts University, I was very involved with the campus evangelism programs. It was during my time as a student at ORU that I established a law in my spirit that weather would never be the determining factor of going on an outreach. I remember on a Friday night outreach in Tulsa, Oklahoma, when only one other brother showed up to go with me. Why? Because it was raining cats and dogs and no one wanted to get wet on a Friday night. I still felt that I had to prove to the Lord that I would go, no matter what obstacles were before me. So we went, and in spite of the rain, we found one man who desperately needed help. When we found that man, the rain stopped, and we ministered to him.

All Christians will be tested on how far they are willing to go for the gospel. Now living in rainy England, I carried the same mentality concerning the weather. The beautiful thing was that God consistently changed the weather for me, and often, after my outreach was completed, the weather would return to the same condition it was before I came.

Several years ago, I bumped into a young French man I knew, and we greeted each other. He told me that he was serving as an assistant in a church in Switzerland. I was so happy to hear that he was in the ministry. He said, "Eric, one reason I went to Bible school and ultimately into the ministry was because I saw you speak to the weather, and it obeyed you. I have never seen anyone speak to the weather. The miracle influenced me towards ministry."

On the occasion he mentioned, the team from Kingdom Faith Bible College and I had arrived in London for the CrossWalk at Easter. The team was a dynamic group of young people from all over Europe. I built the cross, and as we began to walk the weather turned worse and began to rain. I thought: *What's the problem? We never have rain. Surely this will change!* But it didn't change, and I was getting soaked. I instructed the team to head for cover.

Because of our proximity to Parliament and Westminster Abbey, the most suitable place to take cover was the café in the Methodist Central Hall— the very place where I had set up the London Ablaze meetings many years before. The team headed to the coffee shop to grab a hot drink while I sat quietly praying; I was quite perturbed in my spirit. In some ways I identified with the Apostle Paul when the little girl followed them and yelled that these men were servants of the Most High God. Paul could discern the devil in her and was grieved in his spirit. It wasn't until the third day that Paul, through the help of the Holy Spirit, actually dealt with the devil in the girl (Acts 16:18).

On one hand, I was frustrated, but on the other hand, I couldn't help but remember that it all started for me in that historic building. It was at that moment I sensed the Lord encourage my faith. After about an hour I rounded up the team to start walking by faith, hoping that by our going forward the rain would stop. As the team gathered the rain did begin to let up, and I supposed that the weather pattern had changed. But I quickly found out that I was wrong. As soon as we departed from the Methodist Hall the rain intensified, and now I was really perturbed. In an act of desperation, I called the team together, and we gathered around the cross and prayed. We were at the make or break point of either leaving London or continuing with the outreach.

Suddenly, as we stood and prayed, something came down from heaven and the power of God filled me. Being infused with heaven's ability, I looked up and spoke to the weather and commanded it to stop in Jesus' name. Immediately a wind came and hit the weather system above us, causing the sky to open. Within a few seconds the clouds were gone, and the sun shone. In fact, I got a little too warm standing in that sunlight. My French friend said, "I have never seen that before." No sooner had the weather changed that we found ourselves in the midst of a Ghanaian delegation that had come to London to protest in front of the house of the Prime Minister. They had stopped their protest because of the rain, and now, walking in the warm sunlight, they came to us. We were surrounded by a hundred Ghanaians, and the Smile tracts were going out fast. I thought, *How did that happen*? Of course, I knew how it happened, but usually when it does happen we still stand back with our mouths open in awe of God.

The Wind That Blew the Tract

Bradford is a beautiful city in the north Midlands. It was home to the great faith preacher Smith Wigglesworth. On one of my outreaches in this city, I walked up to three young people in their early twenties. While holding the cross I offered them Smile tracts. The first two took them willingly. As I attempted to hand a tract to the third person I hit a wall. This particular young lady was a Goth—completely dressed in black; everything was black. When I tried to hand her a Smile tract she became extremely adamant against receiving it. Suddenly, a strong wind came from behind me and hit my back. When it hit me, I almost dropped the cross and all my tracts. As I struggled to keep from dropping everything, one tract left my hand and blew directly into her hand. Her eyes got big, and my eyes got big. I truly didn't know what to say other than, "Young lady, you can never accuse me of forcing you to take that tract. Furthermore, God is speaking to you, and you need to start listening." As I walked away from her I noticed that it wasn't a windy day, and the placement of the gospel leaflet in her hand was perfect.

No Debating

After I left the three young people I walked over to two young Muslim men. As I witnessed to them an older cleric came over and interrupted our conversation. He was disturbed and wanted to challenge me to a debate. My greatest rule in evangelism is that I will never argue. As a small crowd formed in hopes of watching a religious debate, I quickly shocked them all by saying goodbye. As soon as I turned to leave I bumped into a teenage girl. Within minutes we were praying together, and she received Christ. If I had stayed in the argument I would have missed that opportunity to share Christ with the young lady. The Lord taught me that day never to argue. Throughout the years I have said goodbye to many angry, bitter people.

The Door That Was Locked

Several years ago I took a couple of guys from our home church in Florida to carry the cross in a small town called Apopka. The team and I made our way down the main street and witnessed to everyone we met. Although it was a Saturday morning and many businesses were closed, I could sense the presence of the Lord encouraging me that we were in the right place.

Two of the guys entered a small repair shop and gave out tracts to the workers. As they proceeded to leave they noticed an elderly man sitting in the corner behind the front door. They had not noticed him when they'd walked in. Sitting quietly, with his Bible open, he was busy putting mustard seeds into small packets that had a scripture written on them. The scripture was Mark 11:23, which speaks of faith the size of a mustard seed. Blessed by what we were doing he gave packets to each of us. That little servant of the Lord, hidden behind a door, unnoticed by the world, became a tremendous source of encouragement to us as we walked by faith and sowed the Word of God into that town.

After this encouraging encounter we continued on our journey and came to an office complex. The probability of that particular building being open on a Saturday was slim, but through a glass door I could see people working in the corridor. Sensing a prompting from the Lord I directed a team member to go into the building to give out tracts. After a few minutes he came back with a big smile.

"What happened?" I asked.

My teammate responded, "When I opened the door and went in, the people looked surprised and asked, 'How did you walk through that door? That door is locked!' I was a little shocked, but I told them, 'it was open for me, and by the way, Jesus loves you!'" He gave the tracts to all who were present.

I understood why he was smiling. Though it didn't seem like many people were in Apopka on a Saturday morning, God still had encouraged us by showing us signs of His presence working with us. Over the years, I have realized that God is just as miraculous in the smaller outreaches as He is in the larger ones. In this case, from the mysterious man giving out mustard seeds, to locked doors opening to the touch of our hands, to people repenting and coming back to Jesus, I have learned that all outreaches are important to the Lord, and He is faithful to send His angels to assist us as we labor in His joy-filled harvest fields. By the way, angels love to rejoice over sinners who repent!

> *"Likewise, I say unto you, there is joy in the presence of the angels of God over one sinner that repents."*
>
> Luke 15:10

WHAT IS MAN THAT THOU
ART MINDFUL OF HIM?
PSALMS 8:4

CHAPTER 8

THE FACE OF GOD

In walking with the cross and planting Smile tracts, I often wonder what it must have been like to hear God speak the words, "Let us make a man." I am sure there were angels present, and most likely they were wondering *what is a man*? But the Lord didn't stop there. He continued by speaking words, the depth of which no angel could ever grasp: "In Our image and in Our likeness" (Genesis 1:26). God desired a family, a family of children made in His image and likeness and made to wear His glory. God desired sons and daughters upon whom He could pour out all of His love and glory as a Father, thus making man an heir of all that He had. The angels will never understand the depth of such love!

David uttered the phrase, "What is a man that you are mindful of him?" (Psalms 8:4). I would have loved to have been in the garden, watching as God molded Adam with His hands, like a fine artist sculpting a masterpiece. Perhaps as Adam lay there the angels were wondering, *"What now? It is a very beautiful work, but it is just lying there."* Perhaps one angel suggested, "Maybe we should pick it up and put it by the waterfall to decorate creation?" Then the Lord moved closer and breathed into Adam's nostrils. When the breath of God entered Adam, something happened that caused all of creation to take notice: man was alive. When Adam opened his eyes, the first thing he saw was the face of God. Adam saw his Creator, the Almighty, and when he looked into the face of God, Adam saw God's smile. In the smile of God is everything man needs. He saw love, joy, peace, acceptance, strength, friendship, and so much more.

It must have been wonderful to walk with the Lord through the garden in perfect relationship. I can imagine Adam and God locking arms together and strolling through the earth. As they walked, Adam would name the animals and the plants and everything that he saw. It must have brought great joy to the heart of the Father.

But of course, when Adam and his wife Eve sinned against God, creation changed. Adam's faith had now turned to fear. Adam and Eve had listened and obeyed a different word releasing death to walk in the earth. It was the highest form of treachery committed against the Creator Himself. Sin had infused itself into humanity's nature, and death had become Adam's crown. Creation itself was groaning, now longing and patiently waiting for the manifestation of the sons of God (Romans 8:19).

Where was Adam? When the Lord walked into the garden, He called Adam's name. He knew where Adam was, just as He knows where we are. But as He called out to Adam, His heart was longing for man to come out from the shadows of creation to stand before Him in light (John 3:16-21).

Often as I walk with the cross, I have a tangible sense that the Lord is walking in our midst, calling out to people. It is always such a joy to watch the team go forth from the cross and interact with crowds of people. After a few minutes, I see the bright-yellow Smile tracts go out in all directions as men, women, and children take hold of them. At times I discern the presence of the Lord intensifying as people begin reading the tract.

My father, who has been my cameraman on many London CrossWalks, has captured through the camera lens the change in a person's demeanor as they read through the tract. I personally have watched a quietness of thought come upon people as they read, smile by smile. It is a beautiful thing to watch the presence of the Lord come upon the hearts of men and women. On several occasions I have noticed two people walking together, one engrossed in the attractions of the city, while the other is noticeably drawn away by the message in the tract.

Several years ago, during a prayer meeting for a

London walk, a prophetic word came forth, declaring: "There will be those who, because of their culture and religion, would say, 'This message is not for me,' but when they open the tract, they will see through a portal into heaven and realize there is a place before My throne for them and for their people, says the Lord." Evangelism is simply walking with the Lord into the garden of men's lives and calling out to them. Evangelism is not a method but rather the declaration of a person, Christ Himself.

The Breath of God

One day in Norfolk, England, while walking in the center of that beautiful, ancient city, an Irishman attempted to ride past me on his bike. I called out to him and he stopped. As I talked to him about having a personal relationship with Jesus, I took him through the tract, smile by smile. At the end, he asked me, "Can I be saved if I believe and pray this prayer?" Of course I said yes. He read aloud the prayer of salvation that is written on the back of the Smile tract. At this point I wasn't doing anything but watching the man pray. Sitting on his bike he prayed, then paused, and then something happened that I will never forget. He took a deep breath—or maybe it's better to say that a breath came down upon him. It was the breath of God! The Father is still breathing life into men today.

Then I realized that no man can live, physically or spiritually, without the breath of God.

You Can Save No One

Over the years people have asked me how many people I have led to Christ. When I began this ministry, the Lord spoke to me concerning CrossWalk and FourSmiles. He said, "You will never see the fruit of your labors upon the earth, but when you stand before me, you will see your great reward." Then the Lord set me straight about evangelism with regard to my ability versus His. He continued, "No man can bring another man to Me unless My Father draws him. I have anointed you to bring Me to men." That simple word established a confidence in me concerning my calling, freeing me from the vanity of man's expectations. My calling is to prophesy over nations while plowing and planting the Word of God with a smile!

The Lord made it clear to me that if I obeyed and did what He asked me, my obedience would release others, by the Holy Spirit, to be moved into places of fruitfulness on the earth. There are those who sow, and there are those who reap. The sower makes way for the reaper. In fact, the increase upon the reaping is the same spirit that is upon the sowing. Increase is a spiritual substance in the realm of seed-time and harvest. Many who have walked with me enter into the joy of the Lord as we labor together, planting seed into the harvest of men's lives. If there is joy in reaping, then there also must be joy in sowing! The DNA of any apple tree is the same DNA of its seed. The law of the spirit is seed-time and then harvest.

The Missionary Saved by a Tract

During our years of living in Latvia and working in the Baltic nations, I had the honor of meeting some wonderful missionaries. While visiting in the home of a missionary pastor and his wife, we became engaged in a discussion about salvation. I asked the wife how she came to know Christ. She said: "For many years my friends witnessed to me and prayed for me and I even prayed with them. But nothing seemed to change. One day, someone I did not know handed me a Christian tract. I took it home and read it. Suddenly, everything clicked, and I truly believed that Jesus was the Son of God, and I gave my life to Him."

Then I asked, "How did your husband receive Christ?"

"He read the same tract," she said.

The point I am making is that salvation does not come by a work of the flesh but rather by the power of the Holy Spirit at the right time in a person's heart. As faith-filled Christian disciples we are called to preach, to pray for, and to love lost people. In the final analysis, however, the completed work of salvation is between the Holy Spirit and the individual's heart. You and I, as evangelists, can never change this. Of course, when our words are teamed with God's words, there is no greater joy than to be in on the action of seeing people saved. We are truly called to be co-laborers with the Lord. But with every salvation experience and in every Christian's testimony is an aspect that never changes and is always the same. Sinners who repented heard the word of the Lord in their hearts, and they no longer thought about man, but about Christ and His convincing love.

Do I pray with people to receive Christ? Yes, and I love to do that. But if they don't show signs of desire, I don't push the issue. I know that when I minister to a person, the Lord will speak to his or her heart. I also know that a seed will be planted for a living relationship with Christ. Evangelism is not a method but an encounter with Jesus through the work of the Holy Spirit.

Eve

My wife, Beth, grew up in a home that wasn't one of faith. Her family didn't read the Bible or go to church. One day as she rode home on the school bus, a girl named Eve sat down next to her. Beth didn't know Eve very well, but that didn't hinder what was about to happen. Eve turned to Beth and said with a smile, "Jesus can be your best friend." These words so impacted Beth. Eve's joyful smile was full of light and life.

The next day, as Beth was about to board the school bus again, a young boy ran up to her and gave her a gospel leaflet. She looked puzzled, so the boy responded, "Eve gave it to me and asked me to run it over to you before you got on the bus." This young boy was not even a Christian.

Later at home, while in her bedroom, Beth read the tract. And when she did, the Holy Spirit came upon her, and she believed that Jesus was the Son of God. She became a Christian in her bedroom while she was completely alone; there was no Christian worker present. No pastor in town knew anything about her salvation experience. But God knew right where Beth lived. Today, she is still walking with the Lord.

Eighteen months after praying the prayer of salvation, a friend at school invited Beth to Faith Landmarks Ministries—the very church that hired me several years later, sending me to India via London. That one seed from Eve, the girl on the bus, pulled a lever of destiny that brought a convergence of the plans and purposes of God into the earth.

Don't ever tell me that tracts don't work. The kingdom of heaven is as a man that went forth and sowed seed (Mark 4:26). When seed is released from my hand, the kingdom of heaven goes into operation. That is real power!

We must be very careful that we don't limit God in

what we deem as true salvation. Many people are truly saved, yet they have not connected, for one reason or another, to a local church. It took Beth eighteen months to get to church. The Lord of the harvest knows where these people are, and He canopies over them to feed and protect them by His great love.

He Multiplies Our Seed Sown

To the disciples' natural way of thinking, five loaves and two fish were nothing. To many, the effectiveness of a gospel tract can seem just as insignificant. But to the young boy carrying home twelve baskets full of food, it was miraculous. With God, all things are possible! We must never limit the potential of the Word of God that is written on a gospel leaflet.

Don't Stop Doing What You Are Doing

I was preaching on the streets in the heart of Warsaw, Poland, several years ago when a man came up to me with tears in his eyes. He pleaded with me to never stop doing this kind of ministry. He introduced himself and shared his testimony. He explained that there was a time in his life when he hated Christians like me. Then one day, while walking through the city, a person reached out and gave him a gospel leaflet. He didn't get angry as he usually did; rather, he put the leaflet into his coat pocket, planting it like a seed, awaiting its due season of fruitfulness. Two years later, while going through some very tough situations in his life, he reached a breaking point. One night, under intense pressure, he grabbed his jacket and left the house. Hurrying down the street in a troubled state of mind, he cried out to God, "If you are real, then show me!" No sooner had he prayed that prayer than he put his hand into his pocket and felt the gospel leaflet. When he pulled it out and read it, the Holy Spirit fell upon him, and he gave his life to Jesus. He really encouraged me that day. Everywhere I go in Europe I meet pastors who have very similar testimonies concerning the power of a gospel tract.

It Stuck on Me

Another pastor standing next to me during the previous conversation then shared his own salvation experience. "Many years ago, my friends and I were on a train," he said. "A Christian boarded the train and handed out tracts to every person in the car except me. One of my friends was so angered by the tract that he stood up and threw it, and somehow the leaflet stuck on me. So I opened it and began to read. When I finished reading, the Holy Spirit came upon me, and I believed; I gave my life to Christ. Today I am a pastor." The kingdom of heaven is as a man that went forth to sow seed!

The London CrossWalk

Of all the cities in which I have walked, there is no city like London. From the beginning days, when the Lord stood by me as I walked across Westminster Bridge toward Big Ben until now, eighteen years later, over 900,000 Smile tracts in English, Spanish, French, and Italian have gone out to the ends of the earth from that place. It is the fulfillment of the vision I had at Kensington Temple when I saw spokes of fire and glory coming up from Great Britain and shooting forth to the ends of the earth.

Four Hours Each Day

For our Easter walk in April 2016, I had printed twenty-five thousand Smile tracts for London. On the Friday walk, 14,500 people took the tracts in four hours. It was like a wind came from heaven and blew the tracts out into the nations. The next day we carried the remaining tracts with us, and after four hours 10,500 Smile tracts were gone. In all these years, I have never seen a move of the Holy Spirit quite like that. God created seed, and He is a master at getting it planted!

Throughout my time of carrying the cross, I have witnessed unique happenings that carried the mark, "only God." To experience twenty-five thousand people taking the tracts in eight hours from a team of twenty-five people was extraordinary. Secular companies have asked me what our secret is to getting our brochures out so easily. All I can do is smile when they ask this question.

A Lesson Learned in the Midst of a Miracle

Several years before this, while flying into London for our December walk, a freak snow storm from Russia blew in and covered the south of England in white. Instead of flying to London Gatwick as scheduled, we were forced to land at London's Heathrow Airport due to inclement weather. When the plane landed at Heathrow, we were informed that we could not park at the gate. Fortunately for me, my wife had thrown a hat and a pair of gloves into my carry-on. The flight had originated in Orlando, and unfortunately many of the Europeans on the plane were still wearing their Florida holiday clothes. I felt for them as they froze while walking down the stairs of the plane into the snow and ice.

I usually do an evening prayer and training session on the Thursday before the Friday CrossWalk. During that meeting, the Holy Spirit prompted me to cancel the Friday outreach because of hazardous road conditions due to snow and ice. The thought of cancelling the Friday CrossWalk, turning it into a one day outreach, was very hard for me. Weather miracles have always been a part of the London outreaches, so I struggled with the thought *why couldn't I expect that now?* Yet I didn't sense that I had the faith needed to believe for a miracle that night. Grudgingly, I canceled the Friday CrossWalk and turned to the only thing I had left—dependency on God. For this particular CrossWalk I had printed twenty thousand Smile tracts for an anticipated two-day event in London. Now, my outreach was cut down to one day.

Up until this CrossWalk I had only witnessed one other outreach where 12,500 people had taken the tracts on one very long day. Based upon that result, another 7,500 Smile tracts would still be remaining. I didn't like the math. That night, I spent time praying and seeking the Lord. A gentle prompting came to my heart and I sensed the Lord speak: "I will do in one day what you had planned for two." I became very excited, even though my natural mind was struggling with the realities of the spiritual hardness in the atmosphere in London. I had not forgotten my initial outreach experience during the London Ablaze event years before. It was then that the Lord established in me an understanding concerning my ability and His—that is His ability working through me pertaining to evangelism on the streets of Europe.

I rested on Friday and prepared myself for a one-day—Saturday— London CrossWalk in December. Then I received word from the Bible college that a Christmas carol service in the local town had been cancelled due to the weather. Because of this cancellation, more people were available for my Saturday team.

Then the miracles began. On Friday night a warm rain came upon southern England, melting the snow and ice. The next morning when I woke up, the snow was almost gone, and the roads were clear. Expectancy rose in my heart. When we arrived in central London the weather was clear with absolutely no rain. Later that day people asked about the weather in London and how wet we had gotten. I didn't understand the question. I then realized that it had rained all around London that day except where we were. My heart was so filled with joy, knowing that God had supernaturally moved to make a way for us to plant the nations with the smile of His love.

There was such an ease to that outreach that day. As the team walked back to the mini-buses in order to go home, they asked each other if anyone had more tracts. No one had any left. We had given them all out! We still had one mile to walk, but the tracts were gone. It wasn't until later that I realized that I had failed to distribute all of the twenty thousand tracts to the team. I had foolishly decided to only give them 17,500 tracts due to the logistical reality of carrying twenty thousand tracts around London—not many people want to carry that much weight in a backpack for several hours. As I opened the van doors for the team to jump in I had to face the reality of my own unbelief. I had left one box in the van that could have been planted that day in accordance with the word of the Lord. Although 17,500 Smile tracts going out on the streets of London on a beautiful, dry day was miraculous and carried with it the evidence of the touch of God, I couldn't help being a little ashamed that I had failed to unpack all the tracts; I should have trusted the word the Lord spoke to me two nights before. I stood in the midst of an operation of miracles that had not only touched the people but the weather as well, and I could see that it had been partly hindered by my unbelief. We all do this to the Lord more than we realize. So what should we do when this happens? Keep pressing forward, and don't look behind. Even though we may not do everything perfectly, it is far better to keep walking forward with our eyes on the one who is perfect, and therefore continue to grow in our trust and obedience to the will of His perfect love.

Eric Casto

LIGHT IS SOWN FOR THE
RIGHTEOUS,
AND GLADNESS FOR THE
UPRGHT IN HEART.
PSALMS 97:11

CHAPTER 9

LIGHT CAN BE SOWN

A couple of years ago a church team from Modena, Italy, and I walked with the cross in the ancient city of Naples (Napoli)—such a beautiful place. It is the home of pizza and Mount Vesuvius. The team and I had been working for a couple of hours and were almost out of tracts. There had been such a flow of the Spirit of God upon the tracts causing them to go out so easily. It was in these specific times that we realized that the Lord was working with us and that He loved passing out tracts. When we realized we were almost out of gospel seed, I called the team together around the cross to decide what to do next.

We had more Smile tracts in the van, but I had planned to save them for our outreach the following day in Pozzuoli (Puteoli), the city where Paul landed as he made his way to Rome (Acts 28:13-15). It was then that I noticed a unique-looking man (possibly homeless) walking toward our dear sister Alessia.

Alessia was standing at the far end of the cross, assisting me with the wheel. This man came up and began talking with her, which in turn distracted me from what I was trying to say to the team. As I continued talking to the team, I kept an eye on what was happening with Alessia and the stranger.

Usually I will intervene if I think a situation on the streets may be more than the average team member is ready to handle, but in this situation the peace of God came upon me, and I knew that it was okay. There was such a peace upon that man.

Later that evening I asked Alessia about him. She said: "I was a little concerned when he came up to me, but then I felt assured that it was okay and I didn't need to be afraid." She continued: "There was something special about the man, and there was a peace around him. Then I told him about Jesus and offered to pray for him, and he let me. He was so thankful and then asked if he could pray for me. I replied, 'Well, no, but thank you.' He smiled and then walked away." Everything about him was encouraging.

As I listened to her, a deeper understanding came upon me. It was in that place one year earlier that we had come as a team to do an outreach. When we arrived into the center of Napoli, we found out that a homosexual parade would be coming through that area within the next thirty minutes. The tracts went out quickly, and we already had prayed with many people to receive the Lord. We knew that the

Lord had led us to that place, even though we had no knowledge of the forthcoming event. Police were scurrying everywhere in preparation for a parade that would consist of thousands of Italian homosexuals demanding their right to marry. Somehow, we had been strategically placed in the middle of it.

Everything in me wanted to leave, but we knew the Lord had sent us there. The pastor with whom I was working asked me if he could maneuver the cross closer to the street. He wanted to ensure that the cross was visible to the large crowds of people forming along the parade route. I thought, *Mamma mia, what are we in for?* My team gravitated closer to the cross as the first wave of the demonstrators came past us. Leading the way were small groups of transvestites, advertising different causes. Then the main body of the demonstration arrived. It consisted of thousands of sexually driven people, empowered by an overwhelming, lustful presence. I had never been in such an oppressive atmosphere; it required me to meditate on scripture and pray in the Holy Spirit language to keep my mind in the anointing. (Thank God for that Holy Spirit prayer language!) Toward the end of the parade, thousands of people walked next to a semi-trailer truck with a flat-bed being used as a stage with a deejay interacting with the crowd. Then I noticed there were men dancing on the flat-bed wearing ladies' lingerie. The crowd was loud and energized. But when they saw me and the cross, the atmosphere changed.

The prevailing lust turned to hate. Then the deejay focused the crowd's attention on me and the cross. The crowd responded by pressing in upon us, almost suffocating us. With great anger they cursed and spat at us. The cursing was in both Italian and English, which I found very interesting. I clutched firmly onto the cross for dear life. In this situation we could only trust in the Lord to deliver us. At any moment this crowd could have done whatever they so desired to us, and the police would have been powerless to stop them.

I had never witnessed such hate. I remember thinking that I did not want to be martyred at the hands of thousands of men wearing women's panties. How would I explain that to the apostle Paul when I met him in heaven? After several minutes, which seemed like an eternity, they finally moved on, leaving us emotionally exhausted in their wake. The testimony was that we had survived, but that experience also changed me. Since that parade, I no longer am concerned when one or two people become angry with me and begin to curse at me. After living through thousands of homosexuals mobbing me, ready to tear me to pieces, while cursing and spitting at me, not too much fazes me now.

The Smile tract conveys a message of salvation to all men and not to any one particular group.

Remember that all have sinned and fallen short of the glory of God. In this particular situation, no one from my team said anything about sexual sin; we never had a chance. It was the cross and the presence of God that confronted the spirit energizing that group that day.

Several team members came to me immediately after that horrific event with tears in their eyes. They had never experienced such perversion and hate. They saw people brazenly walking on the road to hell. Regardless of whatever I thought about homosexuals before that event, I walked away having a greater degree of compassion and love for them. Jesus died for all!

One precious sister came to me crying, trying to tell me about something that had just happened. Finally, she gained control of herself and said that a young teenage girl had just asked Jesus to become her Savior. "In the midst of such hate, a person accepted Jesus?" I asked.

"Yes!" she exclaimed. "As I talked to the girl about Jesus, her brother walked over to us and demanded that she leave—but she refused. She wanted to hear more. Finally, the brother became very angry and threatened her, but she still refused to listen to him. Then the young teenage girl said, 'I want Jesus,' so we prayed."

That was happening while I was being surrounded by thousands of homosexuals who were threatening to harm me, but it did not stop God from saving. Even in the midst of such gross darkness, God was operating in light. Remember that darkness is still light to the Lord. During that confrontation the tracts went out so quickly. Many people came up to us in order to take a Smile tract, wondering why we were so hated. Light had been sown into darkness and many heard the voice of the Lord for the first time.

Now, one year later, Alessia and I were talking about the unique homeless-looking man we had met on the streets that day in the same area of the city. We both wondered if that man could have been an angel. The Lord was encouraging us concerning His faithfulness to be with us at all times, past and present. I know that angels delivered us from the demonstrators the year prior, and now I thought, *Yes, it seems the Lord had sent his angel to confirm that His ever watchful eyes were upon us, even in that wicked place.*

THEY THAT SOW IN TEARS
SHALL REAP IN JOY. HE
THAT GOES FORTH AND
WEEPS, BEARING PRECIOUS
SEED, SHALL DOUBTLESS
COME AGAIN WITH
REJOICING, BRINGING HIS
SHEAVES WITH HIM.
PSALMS 126:5-6

CHAPTER 10

BEARING PRECIOUS SEED

It doesn't matter which city I am in or which country I may go to, when I build the cross and put it upon my shoulder the joy of the Lord fills me. There have been occasions when my face actually hurt a little bit from the smile that came upon me. It is sheer joy. Hebrews 12:2 declares that it was for the joy that was set before Jesus that He endured the cross. The cross was a place of complete defeat, yet it was for joy that Jesus endured it, and with that joy He despised its shame. The joy of the Lord is a dominating force that is a real substance of heaven, which the Lord has personally placed into our hearts. The Lord's joy is our strength, and it is designed to empower us as we labor in His harvest fields (Isaiah 9:3).

In the Steps of Paul

And from thence we fetched a compass, and came to Rhegium: and after one day the south wind blew, and we came the next day to Puteoli, where we found brethren, and were desired to tarry with them seven days: and so we went toward Rome. And from thence, when the brethren heard of us, they came to meet us as far as Appii Forum, and The Three Taverns: whom when Paul saw, he thanked God, and took courage.

(Acts 28:13-15)

This passage of scripture touches my heart deeply. The great apostle had narrowly escaped death at the hands of his own countrymen in Jerusalem, only to be handed over to the Gentiles to await trial in Rome. I can't imagine what it was like for Paul to say goodbye to Jerusalem, knowing that he would never see that city again. In the midnight hour, as Roman soldiers whisked him away from the murderous schemes of the religious hierarchy, Paul's thoughts probably drifted back to his childhood years, growing up in Jerusalem and spending much time at or near the temple mount.

The temple in Jerusalem was intricately woven into

the fabric of Jewish life and represented a connection point between the Jewish people, their culture, and their God. Now, Jerusalem was behind him, and a new task was at hand. The Holy Spirit planted Paul as a seed into Rome and, ultimately, Europe. God directed an expansion of His kingdom into the soil of a new continent of people, who would one day carry the message of the gospel to the ends of the earth.

Puteoli (today called Pozzuoli) is the port city where Paul stepped out of the boat onto the Italian peninsula and made his way toward Rome. As the shoreline approached, Paul undoubtedly was filled with intense emotion, knowing that when his foot stepped down into Italy there was no going back. His destiny lay before him at Caesar's judgment seat. Such heavenly courage must have strengthened him to go forward, all the while knowing that his journey for the Lord on earth would end there. He most likely thought back to his missionary travels with Barnabas and Silas and of all the great victories they had won. He must have cherished the thoughts of standing on the beach and praying with the congregations in Asia Minor, while saying goodbye for the last time. The images of men, women, and children—who had once been pagans, but now full of Christ—waving goodbye as he sailed off into the winds of God must have been one of the greatest treasures given to him by the Lord. Truly, these churches were the hidden riches in secret places and Paul had boldly gone to find them (Isaiah 45:3).

As Paul stepped out of the boat, word spread of his arrival. Though, this great apostle had never been there, the believers living in that area of Italy had heard of this man of faith and power. People came from as far north as Rome to meet him and to listen to his revelation of Christ and the power of the gospel. I believe that it left an eternal mark upon that region that is still felt today.

Two Thousand Years Later

The team and I arrived in Puteoli the day after our CrossWalk in Napoli, the outreach where the angel-like man approached Alessia. I had such an expectancy to walk with my cross in that city. Along her streets are ancient temples and markets that Paul would have walked past during his stay. I was greatly encouraged by the Holy Spirit as I walked with the cross, knowing that the gospel is still proclaimed on her streets some two thousand years later.

The team followed behind me, and the smile tracts began to flow out as if a gentle wind was blowing them. I also noticed the ease the team had in witnessing to people. Everywhere we turned, we seemed to find ourselves in in-depth conversations about the Lord. People listened and prayed with us to receive Christ. My heart was touched by a group of young people who wanted to talk with me. Standing with the cross, surrounded by teenagers, I explained why Jesus had to die and be raised again. After explaining the scriptural truths of Christ's love, I then shared my personal testimony of how Jesus changed my life! Those young people listened and then responded by reaching out their hands, placing them upon mine, and praying with me. Truly, it was one of the most memorable experiences on CrossWalk.

The Power of Seed

Over the years, Beth and I have met many people whose lives were changed by a gospel tract. Though some of these people have yet to make Christ their Savior, they still hold dear the little piece of paper with God's message of love. Why? Because when they received the tract, the Holy Spirit, the love of God, touched their hearts. For many, a gospel tract becomes a point of contact for a person to hear the voice of God through His Word. In most cases these people don't hear a physical voice, but they acknowledge that something happens in their hearts when they read it. That burning presence of loving conviction is the voice of God calling out to humanity. That is why we are admonished three times in the book of Hebrews to "harden not our hearts" when we hear God's voice.

Bearing Precious Seed

The key to evangelism is found in the phrase *sowing in tears*. The word *tears* in this passage has nothing to do with emotional pain or sorrow; rather, it is the entry point into the mercies of God. Psalm 126:5-6 is a powerful portion of scripture, as it relates to seed time and harvest. It brings revelation with regard to the need that seed has for water. But the reality is that many places on the earth lack water —places where there are no rivers to water the soil so that seed can take root and grow. It is in these places that our tears of compassion before the Lord on behalf of the lost become the rivers of living water that break forth and water the land.

When the Lord created man, He blessed him and gave him authority, and then introduced him to seed. Man was almost self-sufficient, in that he was equipped with blessing, authority, and seed. The one thing that the Lord withheld from man was rain. We are commanded to ask the Lord for rain in the time of the latter rain (Zechariah 10:1). The need for water keeps man reliant upon the Lord as the source of all increase.

Will You Look at the Lost with Me Today?

I have been on many evangelistic endeavors where the outreach lacked the actual substance of love for those to whom we preach. I remember an outreach in Northampton, England, where the Lord taught me this truth. On the way to the outreach I kept hearing the phrase, "Will you look at the lost today? Will you love them with Me?" At first I didn't know what those words meant, but because I was doing an evangelistic outreach, I thought that constituted the love of God. Evangelism as a method alone is not love. Evangelism is simply proclaiming the good news. Paul wrote that some preach out of envy and others out of good will (Philippians 1:15). Preaching is simply a vehicle that transports whatever is in the heart of the one preaching. Pertaining to God's love—God's love is love!

It was during this CrossWalk that I slowed down and looked at people with the purpose of love. Out of the corner of my eye I saw a young girl sitting alone in an alley. I turned and took the cross to where she was sitting. Alone in that corner of a dirty alley was a teenage girl who was emotionally broken. Her family was dysfunctional, and she had nowhere to live. She said that within the week, she would be heading off to serve time in jail. With a depressed look in her eyes, she poured out her heart and said that jail would offer her a sense of security and boundaries. As the compassion of the Lord filled my heart, I knelt down and ministered to her and then prayed with her to receive Christ. She received Christ in that dirty corner where no one was looking—except Jesus! When we take time to look at the lost with the Lord, we will learn to love them. Without looking at them through the eyes of mercy, we will never truly see them.

Mercy Always Triumphs

Our lives were beautifully changed in May 2003 when we gave birth to our third child, Victoria Faith. Victoria was born with a medical situation that caused her to live in a neonatal intensive care unit (NICU) for the first four months of her life. At that time, we were living on the mission field, far from home and far from family. It was in this death and life experience with our daughter that we had to learn to trust in the Lord, who had promised to never leave us or forsake us.

Beth and I had grown up in faith-believing churches, where miracles of healing were quite common. We knew what the Word of God promised, and we weren't backing down from our confidence concerning our daughter's complete victory. In fact, when the doctor in London had suggested that we abort the baby, the Holy Spirit spoke to Beth from 1 John 5:4, declaring the victory that overcomes the world is our faith. When the Holy Spirit spoke to Beth, she immediately declared that the baby's name would be Victoria Faith. This happened before we knew that our baby was a girl. Even though we believed for a quick miracle, our faith still had to work with patience and the medical staff during that four-month process. I've shared this story because every day when Beth and I opened the door and walked into the NICU at the Saint Michael's hospital in Bristol, we entered into a canopy of mercy and compassion unlike anything we had ever experienced.

We watched doctors and nurses work tirelessly to save lives. Everything that happened in that unit was about caring for those who were the most fragile among us—little, beautiful babies. Every day as we walked to Victoria's area of the unit, we would look at the other children and see the reality of the curse of sin and its disregard for human life. Many times I held back tears as I watched newborn babies fight for a chance to live.

It was in that atmosphere that I learned about the compassion of the Lord. I watched the medical team care for these special little people in a way that I had never experienced at church. Although I had been in many wonderful church services and had witnessed mighty moves of God's power, I had never experienced compassion like this. These trained professionals had positioned themselves to work in the mercies of God as they fought to help every baby live. Even though some nurses were Christians, the majority were not. I learned that the Lord's compassion is available for all to tap into—Christian or not.

In Matthew 25:31-46, Jesus tells the parable of the sheep and the goats. Jesus spoke this parable to refer to those who would be allowed to live and enter into His millennial rule upon the earth. Simply put, those who showed compassion were approved and granted entrance. Those who lacked compassion were immediately sentenced and separated unto eternal judgment. This parable has nothing to do with being born again and going to heaven. It has everything to do with living on the earth and having compassion. Blessed are the merciful, for they shall receive mercy (Matthew 5:7).

I remember the day when we were able to bring Victoria home. She was alive, and we had been changed. Even though I never want to go through that experience again, I will never despise it. I saw compassion on a level that I had never seen, and I was changed by it. After this experience, I noticed that our ministry had also changed. The glory cloud of mercy in which we had lived over those four months was still working in us.

When God's Glory Fills Time

During this time, I took a team to Nottingham, England. The training before the outreach had a strong presence of the Lord upon it, which caused me to become expectant for the actual CrossWalk. When we arrived in the center of the city and began to work, that same presence came down upon us, and I began to preach. After what felt like thirty minutes, a young lady on the team said that she had to go. She said she hadn't anticipated working for four hours.

I looked at my watch and was shocked. What had happened to the time? In that glory of the Lord, time changed. What I thought was a fast thirty minutes actually was four hours. The glory of the Lord in the harvest fields had so infused us that time was not a factor. Remember, the glory of the Lord is not from this world. As to that heavenly atmosphere over which time has no control, I have found that faith operating in mercy and compassion are necessary keys to walking in it. My father-in-law was on that outreach, and we have often referred to it as the outreach where the sense of time was suspended. There are times on the earth when we are given a glimpse of what heaven, saturated in the glory of God, will be like.

God Gives Seed to the Sower

My final thought for you regards the power of praying with compassion for the lost. As we come boldly before the throne of grace, we will find mercy to help in our times of need. It is amazing that the throne of God, full of power and majesty, is called the *throne of grace*, where men find mercy. Flowing from the throne is such compassion, and it carries with it the ability to open rivers in high places to water the land.

As you wait on the Lord, He will strengthen you in order to take hold of seed. Yes, the Lord provides seed to the sower, as well as the power needed to plant and harvest these kingdom operations. He has promised that as we take hold of kingdom seed that He will multiply our seed sown and increase the fruit of our righteousness. It is in this place of sowing that you will find yourself moved by the river of His Spirit into needy places, to sow seed that will release the power of resurrection, causing deserts to become well-watered lands.

After you release your seed, pray and ask the Lord for rain. There in the darkness of the soil, it will seem that all is lost as your seed dies. But, death is not the final story in the process of seed-time and harvest. The very soil that buries your seed will become the source of provision from which your seed will draw as it moves toward harvest. Out of death, your seed will then move into a position of resurrection authority over the soil. As that seed grows, a change will take place where the soil will become servant to the seed and will yield to the seed all that is needed to ensure its fruitfulness. Never underestimate the power of seed!

Don't be discouraged or afraid. The Lord is with you, and He will never forsake you. He will be with you until the end. Be encouraged. Jesus is coming soon, and we must be found ready.

Don't grow weary. For, as we sow to the Spirit of God, we shall reap, and in reaping, we will shine as the stars throughout eternity.

For more information about Eric Casto
and FourSmiles: www.foursmiles.com

Printed in the United States
By Bookmasters